TOXIC HUMANS

Michael Jenkins' Toxic Humans *is a valuable contribution to the discourse on how to work towards more human and more effective organisations. It encourages reflection and suggests concrete ways to address dysfunctionality and toxic behaviour in organisations and to build cultures of trust and psychological safety - which is of increasing relevance given the world we live and work in.*
—Aarti Kelshikar, *Author of How Women Work: Fitting in and Standing Out in Asia*

A timely wake up call for global boards and senior management to level up the leadership playing field. Brilliant management book on how to detox leadership and create better workplaces. Highly recommended insights by the leading global expert Michael Jenkins.
—Martin Roll, Business and Board Advisor, Global Family Business and Family Office Expert, Business School Educator

In Toxic Humans *Michael Jenkins has laid bare some of the dysfunctional behaviour of leaders, past and present. He gives numerous examples of people who cause toxicity in the Boards and organisations they lead and uses his extensive experience to illustrate the different aspects of such toxicity. By analysing the evidence from a wide array of sources he has helped to explain how some CEOs have been able to get away with objectionable management styles for many years. He also has many practical suggestions for dealing with the difficult boss.*

This book should be read by Board Members, whose role is critical in preventing an organisation from going toxic. It is also fascinating reading for anyone with an interest in leadership and how some people occupy positions of power despite their poor interpersonal skills. It answers the question "What is a Toxic Human?", and does a thorough job of analysing the impact on others or "So What?". Finally it proposes ways of minimising the damage caused by toxic leaders and readers who ask, "Now What?" will not be disappointed.

—Peter Thomson, Partner, FutureWork Forum

Work can be inspiring and productive, but when toxic humans are involved everybody loses – even the toxic boss or colleague. Michael Jenkins has done us a service with this thoughtful and detailed analysis of toxic personalities, how they reveal themselves – and what we might be able to do about them. Buy a copy for the toxic human in your life!

—Stefan Stern, former FT management columnist and Visiting Professor in management practice at Bayes Business School (formerly Cass), City, University of London

TOXIC HUMANS

Combatting Poisonous Leadership in Boards and Organisations

BY

MICHAEL JENKINS
Expert Humans Pte Ltd, Singapore

United Kingdom – North America – Japan
India – Malaysia – China

Emerald Publishing Limited
Emerald Publishing, Floor 5, Northspring, 21-23 Wellington Street, Leeds LS1 4DL

First edition 2024

British Library Cataloguing in Publication Data
A catalogue record for this book is available from the British Library

ISBN: 978-1-83753-977-2 (Print)
ISBN: 978-1-83753-974-1 (Online)
ISBN: 978-1-83753-976-5 (Epub)

INVESTOR IN PEOPLE

I would like to dedicate this book to my grandson Henry, a source of great joy for our family.

CONTENTS

LIST OF FIGURES AND TABLES

ABOUT THE AUTHOR

Michael Jenkins was born, and spent his early years, in Malaysia. He graduated from Durham University in Chinese Studies followed by postgraduate studies in Japanese language, politics and economics at Nanzan University, Japan (supported by a scholarship from the Rotary Foundation for International Understanding) after which he worked for Toyota Motor Corporation for four years as a motor analyst in the Overseas Planning Department.

Returning to the United Kingdom in 1988, Michael worked at the University of Bath as the Director of the Foreign Languages Centre where he established and taught on the United Kingdom's first PG Diploma in Japanese/English/Japanese Interpreting and Translation. In 2001, after two years with INSEAD in France as Regional Director, Japan and Korea, Michael returned to Asia as Director of INSEAD Executive Education in Singapore. He subsequently took on the role of Managing Director of the Center for Creative Leadership Asia-Pacific and in 2009 he joined Roffey Park Institute in the United Kingdom as CEO. Moving back to Singapore, Michael joined the Human Capital Leadership Institute (HCLI) as CEO in July 2018 before moving to set up a new company, Expert Humans in April 2020. In July 2020, he joined the UK-based FutureWork Forum (which explores the working world of tomorrow) as a Partner.

The United Kingdom's *HR Magazine* named Michael as one of the United Kingdom's Most Influential Thinkers in Human Resources in 2013 and again in 2016. In 2023, Michael was included as one of the top three HR Influencers in Southeast Asia by *ETHRWorld* Southeast Asia's HR Influencers annual listing. Michael is a regular contributor at conferences in Singapore and abroad where he specialises in topics such as humanising the workplace, new thinking in leadership development, the Future of Work and sustainability.

ACKNOWLEDGEMENTS

I would like to acknowledge the encouragement and support of my Partner colleagues at the FutureWork Forum during the writing of *Toxic Humans*. I would also like to thank the VAB (Virtual Advisory Board) for giving me the chance to explore ideas with its members and for their generous and insightful feedback.

My sincere thanks to Helle Bank Jørgensen, John Barker and Sandra Guerra, for sharing their insights with me about people dynamics in a Board context together with Phaik Ai Choo and Shruti Swaroop, who shared their reflections on people interactions in organisations more broadly. Thank you to Alison Miles, David Fernández Esquivel, Dirk Verbruggen, Gareth Bibby, Jacques Schayes, Jill Davidson, Dr Kiran Chitta, Markus Keiper, Dr Robyn Wilson, Rudi Plettinx and Simon Miles for their kindness and generosity during the writing of this book.

In addition, I am truly indebted to the many brave people who shared their stories of toxicity in Boards and organisations with me: I am also immensely grateful to the many friends and colleagues who volunteered their valuable insights and comments.

I would especially like to thank my wife Joyce Jenkins for the many conversations and her thoughtful insights that helped shape the book. My heartfelt thanks also go to my daughter Maia, son Nat and sister Anna for their support and encouragement.

Thank you.

INTRODUCTION: THE RISE OF THE TOXIC HUMANS

When I was writing my book about altruism, compassion and empathy in an environment of ongoing turbulence – *Expert Humans – Critical Leadership Skills for a Disrupted World* – the alarming degree of dysfunctionality in Boards and organisations I noticed and the disastrous impacts they had and continue to have – made me think about approaching the subject of how to create the conditions for more humane and human workplaces from a different perspective.

I had explored what it would take to create the conditions for more psychological safety in organisations and through doing this, I was confronted time and again by the reality of work life today, which is that too many people are suffering as a result of what we term 'toxic' or 'poisonous' leadership. As I started to reflect on where this toxicity comes from, it occurred to me that while toxicity exists at all levels and in all corners of organisations, it is the Board members and senior management who set the tone for the organisation and who have among their various responsibilities a duty of care to employees who are impacted by the culture that evolves on their watch. It was for this reason that I eventually decided to focus on toxicity in Boards and among senior leaders in organisations – and to start off by asking a trio of questions, namely what exactly are we looking at when we talk about toxicity, what are the implications of this toxicity in Boards and organisations and most critically, what can we do about it, assuming that we *can* do something about it?

We will explore these questions in due course.

And as we go on this exploration it is important to note that when we refer to 'Toxic Humans' we are referring to people who exhibit behaviours that harm or negatively impact other people. It's a term that is growing in popularity, which suggests an increasing awareness – but we need to be alive to the dangers of labelling and our challenge is to try to get beneath the surface of the term 'Toxic Humans' itself. I believe that people are inherently good but that various factors – such as upbringing, environment, systems, context and so on – result in the emergence of certain kinds of behaviour. These factors will be part of the focus of our upcoming exploration.

TOXICITY AROUND THE WORLD

My professional career to date has provided me with the opportunity to experience life in small, medium and large-scale enterprises across the world. This has underscored for me that toxicity transcends local, national and international boundaries. The fact that toxic leadership can show up in subtle and different ways in different cultures adds another layer of interest and complexity to the topic. In addition to working as a full-time employee in a number of different organisations, my work as a Japanese-English interpreter over a period of 10 years provided me with a window on the working lives of different people in different kinds of public, private and not-for-profit organisations – a ringside seat at meetings which were often characterised by breathtakingly cruel behaviour. Today, as a facilitator of leadership and organisational development programmes, I have the opportunity to test and explore assumptions and ideas about toxicity by working with people in a variety of different organisations and asking them about their experiences. So in *Toxic Humans* we will look at how people interact with toxic leaders and what effects these interactions have. We will work towards proposing a way forward that enables employees of organisations to manage and coexist with such toxicity as well as providing some thoughts on how we can contain, mitigate or reduce the worse effects of organisational toxicity. That sounds great, you may say, but isn't toxic leadership something that has been around since the dawn of time, and shouldn't we just settle for the easiest life possible – to keep our heads down and simply try to make the most of a less than ideal situation?

I think this is precisely the problem that we need to tackle: to press the stop button and say unequivocally, enough is enough.

Today there is a growing body of evidence that I will share in due course to suggest that toxic leadership is actually on the rise and that ignoring or tolerating it will result in even more broken lives, more broken societies, more value destruction. One example right now: the UK business magazine *Management Today* cited findings published in the *MIT Sloan Management Review* that 'escaping a toxic workplace culture has now become the number one cause of employee resignations' (22.02.2023). The study analysed 34 million online employees and more than 1.4 million Glassdoor reviews between April and September 2021 and found that toxic workplace culture was 10 times more likely to be the reason an employee would leave their company than their salary. From a Board perspective – where Board members are acutely aware of the role they play in monitoring risk to the organisation – such findings ought to be causing alarm bells to ring. In a world of turbulence, the danger posed by critical talent exiting and the spectre of damage to employer brand as news spreads about the toxicity of the culture – has got to be a reason to pay attention and to come up with an appropriate response.

The good news is that increasing numbers of people are recognising that it is possible to call out outrageous, toxic behaviour and to make progress on tackling it. The challenge that remains however is that people need support and encouragement to call out those often extremely powerful people, scary if not terrifying individuals, who are past masters of intimidation and bullying: they know just how to manipulate others, bend them to their will and leverage systemic weaknesses to further their own agenda. This is not easy, but we will hear stories of bravery later in *Toxic Humans* where ordinary working people went up against toxic leaders – and won.

I am part of an industry that has spent decades looking at the development of leaders in organisations large and small. Thankfully, as key players in the industry, enlightened and progressive business schools have started to evolve in ways that would have been unthinkable 20 years ago – which is to say they recognise completely that it is the *people in organisations* who should be centre stage *as human beings* – and not just cogs in the wheel – while those who lead them must be developed to be effective not just in terms of running a business or organisation, but in ways that ensure their people are cared for and thought about such that *they feel like they belong*. Hence the growing interest in recent years in psychological safety, the critical role of trust in organisational life and the power of learning and development: all of these things give meaning to work and come together, alongside purpose and values, to create a culture. They are intrinsically linked of course (psychological safety, trust and a learning culture) and so to fall short on even one of them can make the difference between being sustainable as a business or organisation or eventually going to the wall.

So, during the course of *Toxic Humans*, we will explore some of the stories of toxic leaders (those leaders who display toxic behaviours) and the damage they have done to their organisations – and countries – and speak to people who have had the misfortune to have worked with or for them – or worse, have managed to get in their way as such individuals pursue power, self-aggrandisement and material benefit. At the same time, we will find that the most dangerously 'toxic leaders' are to be found not only in senior management teams but crucially on Boards as well. 'A fish rots from the head down' is a popular saying and so it is important that we examine the role that Board members play in contributing to the creation of poisonous or toxic leadership, given that such actions have a nasty habit of seeping into the rest of the body politic of the organisation.

I outlined in a recent article for the European Foundation for Management Development (EFMD) and their *Global Focus Special Supplement*, written by the Partners of the FutureWork Forum, that doing more to call out the toxic humans in organisations is long overdue. These individuals are the ones who shape dysfunctionality and normalise what we should all regard as unacceptable behaviour. They are the hardcore bullies, the narcissists and corporate psychopaths who for whatever reason make other people's lives miserable. We need to learn to read the signs and be ready to act against them. Many toxic humans resist coaching: some might say they are individuals who are simply 'un-coachable', and their behaviour goes beyond what we might see as simply incivility. As the following excerpt suggests, I really wanted to press the alarm button about toxic behaviour by human beings in the workplace – because I believe it is vital that we do so:

> They are the ones who use empathy in a negative, nefarious manner thanks to their ability to scent vulnerability in others (usually people who are different to them, gentler or unassuming). These Toxic Humans are the people whose emails, text messages and WhatsApp notifications cause our pulses to race and our throats to feel dry. Does this happen to you at work? Chances are you are the victim of a Toxic Human.
>
> (Michael Jenkins: *The Rise of the Toxic Humans* in Global Focus magazine (2022))

COMBATTING POISONOUS OR TOXIC
LEADERSHIP BEHAVIOURS

History shows that toxic humans and toxic leaders thrive during periods of disruption and chaos, offering as they do simplistic answers to complex issues together with powerful, but unrealisable visions that capture the attention – and endorsement – of people anxious for certainty and 'strong leadership' in a turbulent world.

How indeed are we to combat them, especially in an era such as the one we are living through now?

So let's go deeper by first asking: What exactly *is* a toxic human?

1

WHAT ARE 'TOXIC HUMANS'?

For us to be able to strategise on how to tackle toxic humans effectively, we first have to define what we mean by the term 'Toxic Human'. In her 1996 book *Toxic Leaders: When Organizations Go Bad*, the author and academic Marcia Lynn Whicker described three leadership styles: these were trust-worthy, transitional and toxic. She goes on to define *toxic leaders* as follows:

> *A toxic leader is a person who has responsibility for a group of people or an organization, and who abuses the leader-follower relationship by leaving the group or organization in a worse condi-tion that it was in.*
>
> (Marcia Lynn Whicker, 1996)

I think this offers a useful way to think about toxic leaders – especially the reference to the abuse of the leader-follower relationship. We will return to this later. The idea that toxic leaders leave things worse than they were before is something to which I think we can all relate: we are well aware, for instance, that human history has been scarred by the actions of numerous tyrannical rulers, dictators and politicians – from every corner of the globe. For many of us these people are something more than simply toxic leaders or toxic humans – they are monsters. They have murdered and plundered their way into our collective conscience, demonstrating behaviour that most of us would accept goes far beyond what we might characterise simply as 'toxicity'. The mere mention of Adolf Hitler, Pol Pot and Idi Amin Dada, immediately, fills us with revulsion as we connect these individuals with atrocious and unforgiveable crimes against humanity. Would we have the same reaction at the mention of infamous captains of industry whose actions are reprehensible but who are clearly in a different class of awfulness to the three individuals I have just mentioned? I don't think so. And while there are definitely politicians and business leaders in our world today who arouse strong negative feelings for many people – would we always label them toxic humans? We might actually be tempted to call them sociopaths and narcissists, may be even psychopaths – but as with any kind of attempt to categorise people, we need to take great care with respect to our terminology and characterisations of people. So it is with the term 'Toxic Humans'. In this book, we will use the term to denote people who display the kind of leadership that is poisonous for organisations and whose behaviour undermines, threatens or damages people. In her book *The Allure of Toxic Leaders – Why We Follow Destructive Bosses and Corrupt Politicians – and How We Can Survive Them* (2006), Jean Lipman-Blumen talked about toxic leaders consistently exhibiting toxic traits while routinely engaging in dysfunctional behaviour – and in an article in the *Ivey Business Journal* from 2005, she wrote:

> ...*we can take as our working definition of toxic leaders those individuals who, by virtue of their destructive behaviours and their dysfunctional personal qualities or characteristics, inflict serious and enduring harm on the individuals, groups, organizations, communities and even the nations that they lead.*
>
> (Jean Lipman-Blumen, 2005)

Our task is to try to understand what makes toxic humans – toxic leaders – do the things they do and what, systemically, enables them to *get to do* the things they do. And this is why looking at toxic humans in history can give us some insights into how they came to be so infamous and through this, help us to establish what patterns of behaviour we might need to watch out for in the context of toxic leaders today. We might also gain a better understanding of what has shaped people and perhaps even feel motivated to consider an empathetic or even a forgiving response.

A HUNDRED YEARS OF TOXIC HUMANS IN ORGANISATIONS

As we look back after the last 100 years or so to assess the effect of toxic leaders, there is a discernible trend towards us noticing more – and being able to call out more – their behaviours and actions, something which gives us a distinct sense of something growing in intensity and malevolence. We could name this trend 'The Rise of the Toxic Humans'. But are there really increasing numbers of toxic humans in leadership positions or is it that we just notice them more or hear more about them more often? News travels fast as we know – and bad news travels fastest.

In some ways, the closer toxic business leaders are to us in time, historically – at least in theory – the greater the chances are of being able to analyse and understand their effect on their organisations and even on wider society. The Enron scandal and the actions of the man who presided over the chaos which led to Enron's bankruptcy in December 2001, Ken Lay, have been well-documented and debated. We have a wealth of data to draw on. There are exceptions of course – leaders who were toxic and at the same time ferociously protective of their privacy, which makes it a bit more of a challenge to really know what they were like *to work with*. Were the toxic leaders of the past as toxic as history would have us believe?

Let's begin our journey through time by starting in the late 1890s–1900s to look at some of the controversial leaders of the past.

1890–1900S

Henry Frick (1849–1919) – American industrialist: H. C. Frick & Company, Carnegie Steel Company and United States Steel

Henry Clay Frick was born into a Mennonite family on 19 December 1849 in Western Pennsylvania in the United States. He became an industrial titan and is perhaps most famous for being the Chairman of the Carnegie Steel Company. His family firm, H. C. Frick & Company, formed a partnership with the Carnegie Steel Company led by Andrew Carnegie which resulted in the eventual creation of the behemoth United States Steel. Things turned sour between the two men as a result of their disagreements over the Homestead Steel Strike of 1892: Frick was virulently antiunion and his violent intervention – calling in Pinkerton agents (Pinkerton being one of the earliest detective agencies in the United States, the original 'Private Eyes') to attack the strikers – was condemned by American workers across the country. At one point Frick was labelled 'the most hated man in America'. Andrew Carnegie attempted unsuccessfully to eject Frick from the chairmanship of

Carnegie Steel Company, and even after an assassination attempt in 1892 by the anarchist Alexander Berkman (Frick was shot and stabbed – while the Homestead Strike was still ongoing) – Frick was back in work a week later. As well as being fanatical about hard work, Frick is remembered for being an avid (and skilful) art collector – and it is the nature of his art collecting that gives us a clue as to what kind of man he was and the state of his mental health. In a talk on 22 May 1999 at the National Portrait Gallery in Washington DC, his great-granddaughter Martha Sanger spoke about her book, *Henry Clay Frick: An Intimate Portrait,* in which she explains some of the events going on for Frick that impacted him as a human being, and which resulted – she suggests – in shaping him in such a way that he had *a closer, more intense relationship with his artworks than with human beings.* What drove this behaviour – and explained in a poignant sharing during the talk – was that in 1887 his daughter, eight-year-old Martha, swallowed a pin which (untreated and untreatable in those days) resulted two years later in Martha's abdomen eventually 'exploding in Frick's face'. This led to Frick going through – for the rest of his life – what we might today call prolonged grief disorder (PGD). But the death of the little girl Martha was not the end to Frick's grief. As Martha Sanger explained in her lecture, the 'replacement child' – a little son – died within a week of his birth. The paintings in the Frick Collection reflect Frick's grief – images of how his lost daughter Martha might have looked at different stages of her life, had she lived. There is even a Renoir featuring two sisters, which Frick looked at every day, as a way to remember Martha. In her 1999 talk, Martha Sanger juxtaposes two photographs of Frick – one as a twenty-year-old and the other 30 years on when she says he had become 'hard and cold, and there's a loss of soul' as a result of going through 'nightmarish experiences that you don't even want to think about – when he nearly died twice' on his way to making his first million in the coke for steel business and beyond. He was very successful as a businessman, but his family life was breathtakingly tragic. He was a superstitious man and one can only speculate as to what he felt about his personal family losses, namely the loss of two of his four children: was this some kind of payback for his cut-throat, take-no-prisoners approach to business and the way in which he treated others? Might this have been the source of his toxicity? As Frick recedes into history it is likely (certainly for New Yorkers!) that he will be remembered more for his philanthropy and his art collection – The Frith Collection – than his contribution to the US steel industry or for being a 'robber baron'. For some though, his *contempt* for workers – who he felt were being paid well enough and needed in his view, to work harder – is emblematic of a certain kind of leader: they often despise those they lead, while simultaneously portraying themselves as a great friend to the people. As we continue this journey, we will see this characteristic surface in other businesspeople (https://www.c-span.org/person/?57642/MarthaFrickSanger).

Let us now fast-forward to the 1960s and 1970s.

THE 1960S AND 1970S

Al Dunlap (1937–2019) – American executive: Kimberley Clark, Scott Paper Company, Nitec and Sunbeam

1963 marked the year that Al John Dunlap joined Kimberley Clark as an executive in the company's manufacturing area. It was his first role in the corporate arena following a career in the military. Four years later he joined the family-owned Scott Paper Company. From there he moved to a paper-mill company called Nitec and was president there from 1974–1976. His tenure at Nitec came to an abrupt end, when he was dismissed on account of his aggressive approach to leadership and management. But during his time at Nitec he also oversaw the first of a number of accounting frauds which presaged further accounting irregularities and inappropriate business practices a couple of decades later at Sunbeam, where he became chairman and chief executive officer (CEO) of the company in 1996. It was during his time at Sunbeam that the US Securities and Exchange Commission took legal action against Dunlap, alleging large-scale accounting fraud. By 2002, buried in scandal, and burdened by three acquisitions made under Dunlap's watch that it could not afford, Sunbeam itself went bankrupt.

Dunlap's notoriety made him a favourite subject for filmmakers and writers curious to understand what made Dunlap the human he was. By any reckoning, the term 'Toxic Human' might have been made for him, given that he fulfils Marcia Lynn Whickers' definition of someone who leaves an organisation worse off than when that person first joined said organisation, while exemplifying Jean Lipman-Blumen's definition of such individuals as consistently exhibiting toxic traits and routinely engaging in dysfunctional behaviour. In Dunlap's case, Nitec and Sunbeam both collapsed following Dunlap's involvement with them. He clearly left these organisations worse off than when he joined them. And not only that: his nickname Chainsaw Al was an indication of how as a professional downsizer he saw other people as expendable pawns in a bigger game of corporate chess. When an analyst quizzed him about his business practices in May 1988, Dunlap allegedly said – while grabbing the person by the shoulder: 'You son of a b****. If you want to come after me, I'll come back at you twice as hard'. And an obituary in The Washington Post noted a comment from the journalist John A Byrne, author of the 1999 Dunlap biography 'Chainsaw' who wrote in Fast Company magazine ('Working for the Boss from Hell') that Dunlap:

> ...sucked the very life and soul out of companies and people. He stole dignity, purpose, and sense out of organizations and replaced those ideals with fear and intimidation.
>
> (Harrison Smith, 2019)

Small surprise then that Dunlap was interviewed by the author Jon Ronson for his entertaining and disturbing 2011 book *The Psychopath Test*. And Carol Dweck in *Mindset: The New Psychology of Success* (2016) described Dunlap as thinking that he was 'inherently superior' and her view, an exemplar of the fixed mindset, 'a self-professed fixed mindsetter', a person whose inability to accept feedback from colleagues beneath him and his rabid need to protect his self-image as an infallible 'superstar' (his own word) led to his downfall. John A Byrne in his article ('The Boss from Hell') provides us with an insight from the Harvard Medical School psychologist Martha Stout who notes:

> It goes against our intuition that a small percentage of people can be so different from the rest of us – and so evil.
>
> (Byrne, 2005)

Dunlap himself blithely stated that he recognised psychopathic traits in himself but attributed that to 'leadership and decisiveness' as detailed in Jon Ronson's *The Psychopath Test* and mentioned in Jon Ronson's *TED-Ed talk* (YouTube, 2014). We will reflect more on psychopaths in the next chapter of Toxic Humans.

Let's move on now to the 1980s, which was in some senses the era when the archetypal corporate monsters really began to stir, and to be noticed.

1980–2000

This period was notable for its large representation of controversial leaders: of particular note were John Sculley of Apple, Stan O'Neal of Merrill and Roger Smith of General Motors (GM). Let us take a closer look at Roger Smith.

Roger Smith (1925–2007) – Chairman and CEO of GM from 1981 to 1990

Roger Smith was a GM man through and through, working for the company for most of his life. GM was his top priority, always. Smith had a background as an accountant and rose through the ranks via senior roles in finance all the way to chairman and CEO. He is perhaps best remembered for two reasons: one, the massive restructuring of GM which did not work out and two, the mockumentary on him made by Michael Moore in 1989, *Roger & Me*. I once worked in the automotive industry – my first real job was as a motor analyst for Toyota based at Toyota headquarters in Japan – and one of the core pieces of received wisdom – which was shared by Ford and others – was that it made sense for your vehicles to have a common platform or substrate (where the engineering is the same) while the *external* appearance is subject to great variation in design. It enables you to achieve economies of scale. So things really hit rock bottom at GM when the opposite happened under Smith's watch:

> *The engineering was 180 degrees out of phase. GM cars looked alike outside but were all different inside.*
> (Motor analyst David Cole in Alex Taylor et al., 1992)

Reading that was a red flag for me, to be sure. Digging deeper into how Smith tended to behave, I was intrigued to learn about a particularly confrontational episode with the executive Mort Meyerson where Smith lost his cool in a discussion about a possible merger:

> *The rage that overcame Roger Smith at that instant was as irrational as it was complete, for no one was challenging or arguing with him. …Smith had never displayed publicly the level of anger he*

showed Meyerson that morning, but his close associates had seen it before...It was the rage of a man who regarded himself as all-powerful in the sphere in which he operates, someone who didn't have to accept arguments or rejection.

(Levin, 1989, p. 102)

It reminded me of an interpreting job I did in Los Angeles a couple of decades ago when the big boss of an industrial conglomerate gathered his country managers together to demand of them their projected return on average capital employed (ROACE) numbers for the upcoming financial year (ROACE, a financial ratio that shows profitability versus the investments a company has made in itself). After a long, seething speech about requiring them to go above and beyond the call of duty, and one round hearing from the representatives from different geographies about what they thought their individual businesses could manage, during which time he stared silently into the middle distance as people painfully attempted to manage his expectations, the big boss said that anyone projecting over his threshold of 'x' percent could leave the room – however, for those reporting a *lower* number, he would return in about an hour, after having a swim in the hotel pool, with the expectation that the numbers of those remaining in the room would have been revised 'in a sensible fashion' and therefore more acceptable to him. It was not a great experience to see the panic in the eyes of many in the room as he slowly stood up and sauntered out of the room. This was a classic instance of management by fear. So back to Smith: Smith in contrast to the big boss I have just described, was experienced by those closest to him as an impassive man of relatively few words, a quintessential workaholic sometimes given to making sarcastic comments, so for people to witness explosions of the kind I've just mentioned, would have been truly alarming – not just disconcerting. And here we find one of the cardinal rules of non-toxic leadership behaviour: when people encounter their boss each day they have a general expectation about what to expect, what that boss is going to be like. In other words, from a behavioural point of view, the boss is being consistent. In instances where we find a lack of consistency in our superiors such that we don't know *who* we're going to encounter from one day to the next – well, this is a sure-fire way to destroy any hope of creating the necessary conditions for psychological safety to develop. The story of the demise of Nokia for example is well-chronicled in various business school cases from a strategy/innovation perspective – however the back story – namely the behaviour of the CEO during the period of missed opportunities which weakened Nokia – is not so well-known. In her book *The Fearless Organization*, Amy Edmondson of Harvard Business School paints a damning picture of a CEO who spent most of his time wandering the corridors and shouting at people, thereby destroying any possibility of creating the kind of psychological safety necessary for innovation to thrive. Rather than being the archetypal 'shouty boss', Roger Smith comes across as something of a loner despite a sometimes 'hail-fellow-well-met' demeanour, perhaps happiest with his hunting and fishing buddies – but with a calmness combined with an often-acerbic turn of phrase. According to a report in the New York Times Magazine by Cary Reich on 21 April 1985 *The Creative Mind, The Innovator*, one Smith critic said the GM chairman and CEO 'embodied brilliance unimpeded by humanity'.

So does Smith meet our litmus test of being a toxic human? Well to the extent that his legacy according to Alex Taylor III was 'a fleet of lookalike autos, an unqualified successor, and a mountain of debt that pushed the company close to bankruptcy in 1992' then yes: he left GM worse off than when he joined it (from: Alex Taylor III, 3 April 2013, History's 10 worst auto chiefs, Fortune). It would also appear from what we know that he did not score well on his interpersonal skills either!

2000–2020

Into more recent decades now and what one might call a Golden Period for toxic corporate leaders.

This was a period in time when Enron under Ken Lay made the headlines for all the wrong reasons. At VW, CEO Martin Winterkorn was excoriated for the toxic culture in the company that helped create an environment which was ultimately conducive to the highly damaging diesel emissions scandal. Unfortunately for VW employees, although VW's particular culture was perpetuated and turbocharged under Winterkorn's leadership, the developmental trajectory of VW culture was actually shaped by an earlier figure – the terrifying Ferdinand Piëch. In a conversation with the boss of Chrysler, Bob

Lutz, Piëch was asked for the recipe, the 'secret sauce' for VW's 'success', may be an example of 'How do you do it?'. Piëch offered up the following:

> *I'll give you the recipe. I called all the body engineers, stamping people, manufacturing and executives into my conference room. And I said, "I am tired of all these lousy body fits. You have six weeks to achieve world-class body fits. I have all your names. If we do not have good body fits in six weeks, I will replace all of you. Thank you for your time today.*
>
> (Edmondson, 2018, p. 57)

Interesting approach. As Amy Edmondson points out, this is a 'textbook example of how to create a psychologically unsafe environment while seeking to motivate' (Edmondson, 2018).

And there were other leaders making their mark at this time too: one of them was Carly Fiorina.

Carly Fiorina HP (b. 1958) – American executive, former CEO of Hewlett-Packard (1999–2005)

Cara Carleton Sneed was born in 1958 in Austin, Texas. Her mother was a painter of abstract art and her father, a law professor. Carly had a remarkably international upbringing, attending school in the United Kingdom and Ghana before completing her high school years in North Carolina and eventually gaining her BA in philosophy and mediaeval history from Stanford University. After her MBA studies she landed a job with AT&T before moving to Lucent and eventually to Hewlett Packard in July 1999. Writing in Fortune magazine years later in 2015 ['Carly Fiorina as a Boss: The disappointing truth'], Jeffrey Sonnenfeld of the Yale School of Management characterised her ascendance as something enabled by,

> *.... a dysfunctional HP Board committee, filled with its own poisoned politics... [hiring Fiorina as] a CEO with no experience [and] no interviews with the full board.*
>
> (Sonnenfeld, 1999)

Not exactly an auspicious start – and an example of how systemic weaknesses in organisations can facilitate the rise of the toxic leader. So what was Carly the Boss like to work for?

Well, she certainly had an appetite for early morning meetings and often worked late into the night – and expected her people to do so too. In that respect she is recognisable as a typical 'driven leader'. Sometimes going along for the ride with a driven leader is exhilarating. But it is hard to sustain that level of speed – and commitment. Burnout can be just over the horizon. So let us look a bit deeper into what ultimately helped contribute to Fiorina's eventual downfall.

One of the biggest challenges for Carly Fiorina in a company like Hewlett Packard was that she really needed to create connectedness with the amazing engineering brains in the company as soon as possible early on in her tenure at Hewlett-Packard (HP). Unfortunately, this is something that in retrospect she seems not to have achieved. For a person with a sharp strategic mind, it seems odd that she did not work this out. My sense is that she might *not have been able to do this,* i.e. she may have lacked the human skills necessary for getting close to those technical experts. Was she able to empathise with them, at least from a cognitive if not an emotional, affective empathy standpoint? Did she appreciate the power of people *without* positional power to influence events? Whatever the reason, her approach did not play well. Carly's strength lay in her ability to lead from the front and to be an extremely effective communicator. Taking centre stage came naturally to her: in retrospect, it might have been a good move to have focused on her significant strengths by hiring a chief operating officer (COO) to take on the more operational aspects of the job, thereby leaving Carly to do what she did best, which was to promote the company to the world outside and to leverage her significant talent as a strategist. Instead, she concentrated on promoting Brand Carly as part of a HP outreach strategy, but failed to spend time back at the ranch forging those critical friendships I have just mentioned. This effectively meant her leadership position was built on foundations of sand. And despite her appearances as a leadership guru at various events today, where she extolls the virtues of teamwork, it seems that this was not the coda she adopted at HP. The picture you get is one of a voraciously ambitious person whose ego was something to behold. And talking of pictures, I thought it interesting to learn from my research that in her early days at HP, Carly had her portrait hung at the entrance to the HP headquarters alongside founders Hewlett and Packard, a move heavy with symbolism that would not have been well-received by many in the company. The ego had landed (Waters & Chon, 2015).

But perhaps the most interesting thing about Fiorina, seen through the lens of toxic leadership, is that she appears to have been inconsistent in her interactions with her people. She could be warm-hearted and approachable one day and cold-hearted and distant the next. In this regard she is another example of the kind of boss people find hard to read and whose behaviour is difficult to understand (let alone manage). Most people yearn for consistency in their bosses and the message is clear: people get anxious when their boss turns up each day as a different person!

Finally, in an interview with *The CEO magazine* (10 October 2022, '*Exclusive Interview with Carly Fiorina: "I was overlooked and dismissed"* by Michael Wayne'), Fiorina shares the following advice:

> *I don't care who the leader is, they don't know it all, they can't do it all, and they can't fix it all on their own. Humility is an absolute requirement, and if occasionally a leader feels as though they don't appear big and tough all the time, honestly that's a small price to pay.*
>
> (Wayne, 2022)

Humility. Perhaps with the passage of time and the benefit of reflection, humility is something that Carly Fiorina has learnt is an important aspect of good leadership – rather than appearing 'big and tough all the time'. At the same time, her comment is suggestive of someone who has spent a great deal of time thinking about how to 'appear big and tough'. It is this aspect of appearing 'big and tough' that I think was the hallmark of the business leadership of the 2000s, and while we still see it looming large in politics, I would like to think that business leadership is now more open to considering a different way of being and showing up. And even though 'big and tough' is past its sell-by date in many cultures, of course it persists in many others. This is where Boards can play a critical role in bringing about a change in leadership style – towards a 'non-toxic' style. For example, there have been instances in recent years where Boards have put a stop to manifestly toxic behaviour on the part of the CEO – cases include Travis Kalanick at Uber – but other leaders still proudly persist with leadership behaviours that are looking increasingly out of place and out of touch. Another issue raises its ugly head: while Boards may be able to root out toxicity in the senior management – what happens if the genesis of the toxicity is the Board itself? We will return to this question later (Wong, 2017).

But in the meantime, while all the leaders we have looked at so far have come from the United States, what about the *rest of the world* and its toxic leaders?

Examples from outside North America
Gerald Ratner – (born in 1949) – British businessman, Ratners Group

Someone who made the news in the 1990s – for all the wrong reasons – was CEO Gerald Ratner. Ratner managed to destroy his jewellery retail business in a single after-dinner speech to the gathered great and good of British business back in 1991. When asked for the secret to his business success, Ratner jovially described his products as 'total crap' that could be sold at high margins – where earrings in his stores cost 'less than the price of a Marks & Spencer prawn sandwich' – and where 'the prawn sandwich would probably last longer'. He thought it a hilarious speech but unfortunately his loyal customers – those people of modest means, boyfriends, girlfriends, engaged couples – did not. They did not see the funny side of it at all. They did not like being made figures of fun, and so as customers they left in droves – and the Ratner business collapsed. This whole sorry debacle has come to be known as the 'Ratner Effect'. Ratner today makes speeches about this famous episode in British corporate history and how he learnt the hard way that it is not a good idea to ridicule your company's products (at least not in public!) So was this an example of toxic leadership? I think it would be harsh to characterise it as toxic per se but it is certainly a great example of leadership hubris – and it definitely meets the criteria of leaving your organisation in worse shape than you found it (one of our 'toxic leadership' markers). In this famous case, Ratner inherited a lively business from his father and managed to completely destroy it. Unlike other leaders who caused an existential crisis through a particular behaviour (in this case, recklessness), Ratner learnt from his mistake and took responsibility (Buckingham & Kane, 2020).

Mike Ashley (born in 1964) – British businessman, Sports Direct

Admitting your mistakes and taking responsibility for them (like Ratner did) is not the usual behaviour of toxic leaders. They normally blame everyone other than themselves when things go wrong. Mike Ashley of Sports Direct presided over a storm of controversy during the time he was in charge of Sports Direct (he is still the biggest shareholder) and was said by British Members of Parliament (MP) to be directly accountable for creating an organisational culture that exploited its workers and treated them inhumanely:

Workers at Sports Direct were not being paid the national minimum wage, and were being penalised for matters such as taking a short break to drink water and for taking time off work when ill. . . Serious health and safety breaches also seem to have occurred. For this to occur in the UK in 2016 is a serious indictment of the management at Sports Direct.

(SHP Safety and Health Practitioner: Sports Direct treats workers 'as commodities rather than human beings', newsletter, 22 July 2016)

Under close and repeated questioning by MPs, Ashley continued to maintain that he was 100% 'unaware' of any of the issues outlined.

One *good* thing – if it could be termed a good thing – is that the Victorian workhouse conditions at Sports Direct (the 'business model' of Mike Ashley) and his role in creating them – triggered a wave of condemnation in Britain and added impetus to demands that Boards should take a much more active and applied role in creating and overseeing culture in organisations. Research by the Chartered Institute of Internal Auditors noted ominously in 2016 that:

Nearly one in three (31%) of boards across the public and private sectors have not established or articulated what sort of corporate culture they want and only around a third (36%) assess the extent to which values are manifested in the behaviour of all staff within the organisation.

(Medland, 2016)

Many on Boards will take the view that *oversight* of the culture, rather than the actual *shaping* of the culture, is what they should be doing. I think it is a delicate thing to get right. We will discuss this topic in more detail in Chapter 6 when we consider the question: 'Now what?'

In this chapter, we started the work of defining the term 'Toxic Human', with a look at some of the big, controversial personalities of the past. In thinking about whether Toxic Humans are made or born, my working assumption is that they are formed of a mixture of things, and we will dive deeper into this in Chapter 2.

It is intriguing to speculate about what more these leaders might have achieved had they been able to manage or tame some of their often-self-destructive behaviours. Such speculation is only really helpful for future leaders of course if it helps us to see patterns (potential 'derailers') that we can anticipate sooner and which enable us to take the appropriate mitigating action.

The world of politics seems to throw up an inordinate number of people whose behaviour we fail to challenge quickly enough. Take the spectacular fall of none other than the Deputy Prime Minister of the United Kingdom, Dominic Raab. An investigation into allegations of bullying of civil servants by Raab, carried out by Adam Tolley KC, found that:

> ...Raab acted in a way that was intimidating by way of "an unwarranted and persistently aggressive conduct", and that he introduced "an unwarranted punitive element."
> (The Observer Editorial, 23 April 2023)

Tolley also stated that the civil servants who came forward to complain were 'acting in good faith and were "sincere and committed, with no ulterior agenda"' (The Observer, 2023).

Raab resigned, saving Prime Minister Rishi Sunak the embarrassment of sacking a key ally. It is worth underscoring the fact that this was a scandal involving bullying and intimidation at the highest levels of government, proving that toxicity can, and does, go right to the top. As The Observer goes on to note, this is not an isolated incident of unacceptable behaviour:

> Raab is the third senior minister to be forced out of Sunak's cabinet in the first six months of his premiership: Gavin Williamson resigned last year over allegations he had told a civil servant to "slit your throat", and Nadhim Zahawi was sacked in January [2023] as a result of failing to declare that the HRMC [tax authorities] were investigating his tax affairs. Sunak reportedly knew about the allegations hanging over these three men when he appointed them.
> (The Observer Editorial, 23 April 2023)

This is a good example of knowing about toxic behaviour but choosing to do nothing about it.

DISCERNIBLE PATTERNS IN TOXIC HUMAN BEHAVIOUR

We will add more to our emerging list of characteristic of toxic leaders as we progress with our exploration. For now, with our examination of some historical toxic leaders as well as more contemporary individuals, we get a picture of people who:

- Have a laser-like focus on self-promotion;

- Are often charismatic;

- See other people as tools to exploit on their way to the top;

- Have an inability to be contrite;

- See themselves as right all the time (even as they espouse the need to solicit other views);

- Are inconsistent in their behaviour towards others;

- Have low levels of self-awareness;

- Use empathy not to connect with people but to access vulnerabilities in them.

We will gradually augment this set of features and start to see what elements come together to create poisonous leadership. Once we have sized the problem we can start thinking of ways to tackle it.

OTHER FACTORS

The other major force at work is human systems, and the question to ask is: to what extent do human systems themselves foster and perpetuate toxic leadership in organisations? What is it about toxic leaders who draw us like moths to a flame? We will examine these questions shortly.

In concluding this chapter, perhaps we should mention one of the most famously controversial leaders of recent times – Steve Jobs. In my classes, participants often challenge my advocacy of compassion and empathy by saying that Steve Jobs had none of those things but was hugely successful. So who is right when it comes to defining a successful leader? Well, I have to say that I am drawn to the view so eloquently expressed by Ray Williams in his article for The Financial Post on 12 April 2012 *Why Steve Jobs is not the leader to emulate*, where Williams says:

The concern I have, and that is reflected by other leadership experts, is the faulty cause and effect, and "ends justifies the means" arguments that hold up Jobs as a leader to be emulated. It goes something like this: It doesn't matter what kind of boss you are – meaning abusive – as long as you get results (financial); and as long as you attain your goal (financial results), any methods to get there are okay, including abusing people.

(Williams, 2012)

Ray Williams expressed this view over 10 years ago. Unfortunately, in the time that has elapsed since then, workplaces across the globe continue to be dominated by toxic leaders. At the same time, I believe there are some encouraging signs that people want a change towards a different kind of leadership. The challenge is how to speed up that process: to not waste time. As I have found in my career, procrastination in the face of difficult decisions is a terrible place to be: as a leader you are often the only one who can effect a change (such as exiting a bully) and until you do, people will continue to suffer at the hands of those bullies, those humans displaying toxic behaviour.

Intriguingly however, writing in *The Economist*, Bartleby offers up a word or two of caution when it comes to exiting what are termed 'jerks' in the article 'A zero-tolerance approach to talented jerks in the workplace is risky':

...the enthusiasm for banning jerks ought to make people a little uneasy, for at least three reasons. The first is that the "no-jerk rule" involves a lot of subjectivity. Some types of behaviour are obviously and immediately beyond the pale. But the boundaries between seeking high standards and being unreasonable, or between being candid and being crushing, are not always clear cut. Zero tolerance is dangerous. You may mean to create a supportive culture but end up in a corporate Salem, without the bonnets but with the accusations of jerkcraft.

The second is that jerks come in different flavours. Total jerks should just be got rid of. But they are rare, whereas bit-of-a-jerks are everywhere and can be redeemed. The oblivious jerk is one potentially fixable category. Some people do not realise they are upsetting others and may just need to be told this much.

Other people are situational jerks: they behave badly in some circumstances and not in others. If those circumstances are very broad (whenever the person in question is awake say), then that tells you the problem cannot be fixed. But if jerkiness occurs only specific moments, like interacting with another jerk, then it may be that a solution exists. If the thing that a talented jerk does really well can be done in comparative isolation without giving them power over other people, consider it.

> *Then there's the well-known philosophical teaser: if a jerk throws a tantrum in their Home Office and no one is around to see it, are they really a jerk?*
>
> (Bartleby, The Economist, 2023)

We will explore jerkiness/toxicity during the course of Toxic Humans and, given the 'different flavours' referenced here by Bartleby in *The Economist*, think about the various nuanced ways in which we will need to combat, deal with – or contain – these individuals.

2

WHAT CAUSES HUMANS TO BE OR TO BECOME TOXIC?

In this chapter, we will start to explore what causes humans to be or to become toxic, and how this toxicity or toxic behaviour manifests itself – the characteristics of human toxicity. We will try to assess how prevalent toxic humans are in our organisations today. We will also consider the idea that toxicity itself is a part of continuum which includes psychopathic, sociopathic or narcissistic behaviour. Do 'corporate psychopaths' really exist – or are they part of our urban mythology?

Let's find out.

TOXIC HUMANS IN POPULAR CULTURE

Our experience of toxic humans from literature and film has helped to shape our notions of what bad, evil and toxic people look like. When you think about it, what villains from books or movies do you recall from your childhood? Who do you remember most? As a child, I was a little late to the party when it came to bad people from animation or film because I spent a number of years in Africa where we did not have TV or cinemas. Of course, it was pre-DVD and pre-internet as well! Returning to attend boarding school in Britain in the early 1970s presented some opportunity to catch up – usually during school holidays or short breaks when I went to stay with relatives in Wales because like everything in British boarding schools in the 1970s, television ('telly') was strictly rationed. In common with many youngsters, I was a voracious reader, and at school, I particularly enjoyed our English literature classes. It was through reading classics like *Oliver Twist* that I came across people like Bill Sykes, the killer of the angelic Nancy. Later, we were introduced to other novels like *Lord of the Flies* – which was truly shocking in its intensity, especially for me and my friends since we were roughly the same age group as the boys in William Golding's seminal work.

During my teens, my family and I were frequent visitors to the house of my uncle and aunt, who lived in the South Wales coastal village of Llantwit Major. Theirs was a beautiful, multi-storied old townhouse, modernised in such a way that it reflected the owners' time spent in Canada and the United States, with furniture and artwork from North America and jazz playing constantly in the background. But the best thing of all was that my uncle and aunt had a wonderful library of British and American books thanks to my uncle's profession – that of lecturer in English and American literature – and the couple's shared love of fiction. I spent hours in their library and as my cousins and sister grew up, and later my own children, they did too. As a family, I think we developed into people who are curious about what makes people human – and what makes them do the things they do. Through the books in that library, we absorbed details about all sorts of people from all sorts of backgrounds — and spent many hours at the dinner table as kids – with the adults – debating about the world and the people in it – good and bad.

Later, I studied French, German and English as an older teenager and through these studies encountered what some might consider pretty esoteric writers such as the French Roman Catholic writer François Mauriac whose greatest novel was *Thérèse Desqueyroux*, an astonishing psychological study of a woman accused of poisoning her husband (unsuccessfully) and the ensuing closing of ranks by the wealthy family who, eager to avoid publicity or controversy, engineer a cover-up. But mainly, it concentrated on the mental state of the main female character and made me think about things I had never come across or thought about before, such as a totally debilitating nihilism and inability to react to events at all – the theft of identity and agency of one human by another. It was baffling for me as a person in their late teens to try to make sense of what was going on in the head of the damaged Thérèse and, at that time, a real stretch to grasp the toxicity of her situation and the actions of the people, especially her husband, Bertrand, in exacerbating her suffering through psychological bullying.

Then there was of course the novelist Franz Kafka, and here I am thinking less of his most famous works and more of his short stories. One in particular, *Ein Hungerkünstler* (A Hunger Artist) has stayed with me all these years: it's about a circus performer who starves himself as a spectacle for visitors – a popular voyeuristic pastime for circus-goers for more than 200 years (even stretching into the early twentieth century) – which basically involves staring at someone who is starving. The hunger artist eventually dies, forgotten in the straw of his enclosure, and gets quickly and unceremoniously disposed of by the circus hands, to be replaced by a panther, which is altogether more popular with the crowds than the (now) boring hunger artist. It's a parable or metaphor for a kind of unbridled pride, an almost narcissistic kind of behaviour (the idea of the hunger artist being that as an expert in his art, he can go on, and on, without eating: literally, dying for his art). I was struck by the sadness, bleakness and lack of humanity in this short story: the notion that no one really cared. Kafka's blunt message was that the man died for his art: and that doing so was pointless in the end – since no one noticed – evidence if you like of a toxic, unfeeling society and era.

My aim in sharing these two examples from literature is to underscore something that gradually started to dawn on me as I exited my teen years. How strange it is, what goes on in people's heads!

I guess this is why I enjoy, and laugh, at every remembering of the exchange between the young lion Simba and his villainous uncle Scar in Walt Disney's *The Lion King*:

SIMBA: You're so weird!
SCAR: You have no idea.

And I think that's an important point. With toxic humans (or lions), what *is* going on in their heads?

PSYCHOPATHS, SOCIOPATHS AND NARCISSISTS

I have spoken to many people who have described their suffering at the hands of toxic bosses (and toxic teammates). One person declined to be interviewed because the treatment they received at the hands of a highly narcissistic individual was something they did not feel they wanted to revisit. Almost as a throwaway remark, people who have suffered will say things like: 'He was so awful that I think he must have been a psychopath'.

The word 'psychopath' has come to mean, for many people, the epitome of cruelty and callousness – not to mention associations with insanity, madness and horrifying violence. From literature and movies, we have Anthony Hopkins' Hannibal Lecter as possibly one of the most famous 'made-up' psychopaths – and then we have the truly terrifying real-life psychopaths, people like Ted Bundy and Aileen Wuornos, played by Zac Efron and Charlize Theron, respectively, in the films of these murderers' lives.

So when people talk about toxic leaders as being 'like psychopaths' – what do they actually mean?

ROBERT HARE'S PSYCHOPATHY CHECKLIST REVISED (PCL-R)

In his fascinating book *Making a Psychopath: My Journey into 7 Dangerous Minds*, Dr Mark Freestone explains the significance of the PCL-R. This was:

> The gold standard psychopathy assessment used by forensic psychologists and psychiatrists across the world, which consists of 20 items relating to distinctive traits of a psychopath, each rateable between zero and two. If we take the more conservative threshold used in the United States, someone needs a score of 30 on the PCL-R to be diagnosed as a "clinical psychopath"; this means, as Jon Ronson points out in his terrific book on the subject of the PCL-R – The Psychopath Test, that there are 15,504 different combinations of items that would result in someone meeting the threshold, each representing a different cluster of different traits: over 15,000 different ways to be a psychopath.
>
> (Freestone, 2020)

Significantly, in his revised edition of the original Psychopath Checklist, Bob Hare incorporated criminal and behavioural characteristics into the new PCL-R. As Mark Freestone points out:

> In many respects this was a great decision: it's allowed the checklist to be used in courts, where it was not just an assessment of a clinical condition but, as a hybrid measure, could also perform a fair assessment of a convicted offender's chances of reoffending. However, it also leads to a fundamental change in the way we think about psychopaths, from people with a moral deficiency similar to

madness, to people who are primarily criminals whose emotional and thinking deficits make them more suited to and predisposed to crime.

(Freestone, 2020)

Bob Hare's work has without doubt divided people. Here's what Willem H.J. Martens of the W. Kahn Institute of Theoretical Psychiatry and Neuroscience, writing in Medicine and Law, YOZMOT 2008 in the pages of the Forensic Psychiatry section had to say:

The Psychopathy Checklist Revised (PCL-R, Hare, 1998a) is presented as a useful instrument for assessment of psychopathic personality disorder or psychopathic traits and prediction of violent behavior, and recidivism. He [Robert Hare] believes that psychopathy is a distinctive and useful diagnostic category, although the term is rejected by official psychiatric and psychological organizations and is excluded from current diagnostic manuals such as DSM-V (American Psychiatric Association, 1994). The current official term is Antisocial Personality Disorder (American Psychiatric Association, 1994). Most alarming is Hare's conclusion that people who are diagnosed with his instrument (PCL-R) as high…. are untreatable (Hare, 1998b; Hare et al., 2000). Hare even claims that psychopaths even actually get worse with [the] help of psychotherapeutic treatment (Hare, 1998b; Hare et al., 2000). He actually discouraged forensic psychiatric teams to treat psychopaths (Hare, 1998b; Hare et al., 2000). However, many prominent investigators, specialists and therapists challenge these conclusions of Hare and his colleagues and the usefulness and reliability of his checklist… It is also very alarming that Hare's opinions are widely accepted and applied in the forensic psychiatric world.

(Martens, 2008)

Willem Martens leaves us in no doubt as to where he and the American Psychiatric Association stand on this point. He refuses to recognise 'psychopathy' as 'a distinctive and useful diagnostic category', something that would seem to be borne out when I explored an interesting book called *Pediatric psychopharmacology* to see what the thinking was on administering drugs to children with a mental illness and, given the bewildering number of drugs and the equally bewildering number of diagnoses of mental disorders, I was also curious to see whether 'psychopath' or 'psychopathy' would feature in a book on drug therapy for small children and adolescents. The book, an amazing (and heavy) work, edited by André Martin, Lawrence Scahill, Dennis So Charney and James F. Leckman, all with US institutional affiliations (published by Oxford University Press), did not include any such terms or references.

Like many of my colleagues in the leadership field, I am curious about psychometrics in general – and I'm a great fan of lists. In the Human Resources community, assessing competencies and measuring people's ability and potential – is a massive area. So I am somewhat disappointed that not everyone is positively predisposed towards the Hare Psychopath Test, as it seemed a handy way to think about psychopaths. Nevertheless, it also struck me that it gives people like us – in the workplace – the possibility of discussing someone not as a *high-scoring psychopath* necessarily but more as to whether they demonstrate particular traits that are often *associated* with people who see the world very differently to non-psychopaths. That feels useful. And it seems logical as a next step, therefore, to start thinking of people (and their 'toxicity') as being on a kind of multi-layered continuum where toxicity can merge with psychiatric disorder or dysfunction at some point. I mention 'multi-layered' continuum because clinically defined psychopaths, as we know, come in all shapes and sizes. Being a psychopath doesn't automatically make you a criminal after all. As Mark Freestone explains:

> There are a fair number of people in the community who would not meet the criteria for criminal psychopathy on the PCL-R but do have a lot of the emotional or affective and interpersonal features that make up a major part of psychopathy: lack of remorse, pathological lying, glib and superficial charm, conning and manipulative – but none of the antisocial elements. These are often called "successful psychopaths" – successful in the dual sense of both succeeding at life but also perhaps not having been caught doing anything criminal – and they may make up 3.5% of people in the business world. How concerned should you be about a psychopath who is no more likely than a non-psychopath to commit violence? Certainly successful psychopaths are often experts in relational aggression, bullying, and controlling behaviour designed to damage people's social status, but there is also some evidence that these people are different from criminal psychopaths in fundamental aspects of their brain

function. As well as a higher IQ, in some studies higher than the population average, and less impairment in the areas of their brain typically associated with criminal psychopathy, they often have high levels of cognitive empathy – that is the ability to recognize emotion in others without feeling it.

(Freestone, 2020)

The italicized words in this passage (mine) are the key to how we might want to think about the connection between psychopaths and toxic board leaders and senior managers in organisations. It's often puzzled me as to why people will nonchalantly agree that psychopaths 'don't do empathy'. The fact is, however, that many *do* achieve empathy – cognitive empathy that is, not emotional or affective empathy. To give you an example: I once had a visit from a leader from overseas who was not known for his great people skills. When we discussed team-building strategies and I said our team would occasionally go out for drinks and snacks on a Friday evening, to relax and joke about work and gossip about the big bosses – which all helped to build cohesiveness within our team – he looked at me, mesmerized, as if to say: 'That is truly amazing'. I didn't think it was amazing at all – just something that ordinary people do when they are bonding in a group setting. I could see that from a purely emotional standpoint, he really didn't 'get it', but by using his considerable intellect – his 'cognitive empathy' – he suddenly began to 'see' or 'feel' why this simple act of humans socialising might actually be desirable. And with that, he harrumphed with a 'Well, whaddaya know? I am going to suggest these Friday night get-togethers to the folks at HQ – we should try them!'

He seemed well-pleased at making this amazing discovery about people.

PSYCHOPATHS AND SOCIOPATHS

In an article in Medical News Today (6 July 2021 by Anna Smith Haghighi), the writer notes how people often use both terms (psychopath and sociopath) interchangeably. In this medically reviewed piece, we read that:

– *"Sociopath" is an unofficial term to describe a person who has antisocial personality disorder (ASPD), whereas psychopathy describes a set of personality traits. However, ASPD and psychopathy can overlap.*

(Smith Haghighi, 2021)

We know that the American Psychiatric Association uses the term 'Antisocial Personality Disorder (ASPD)' and not the terms 'psychopathy' or 'psychopath'. So when we hear that ASPD and psychopathy can 'overlap' – what does that mean? Anna Smith Haghighi goes on to explain the symptoms, and I have rendered these in a table whose items we will refer to during the course of this book.

To get a sense of scale, here are some fast facts about ASPD and Psychopathy:

- *ASPD occurs in about 1–4% of people* (United States National Library of Medicine, PubMed Central, Antisocial Personality Disorder by Kristy A. Fisher, last update 15 August 2022).

- *ASPD more likely occurs in males* (United States National Library of Medicine, PubMed Central, Antisocial Personality Disorder by Kristy A. Fisher, last update 15 August 2022.

- *Healthcare professionals would classify only 1% of the US population with psychopathy using Hare's Checklist* (United States National Library of Medicine, PubMed Central, Psychopathy: Developmental Perspectives and their Implications for Treatment by Nathaniel E. Anderson and Kent A. Kiehl, 9 February 2015).

- *Approximately 20% of people in prison in North America would meet the criteria for psychopathy* (United States National Library of Medicine, PubMed Central, Psychopathy: Developmental Perspectives and their Implications for Treatment by Nathaniel E. Anderson and Kent A. Kiehl, 9 February 2015).

Given these numbers, and thinking about a 'toxicity into psychopathy' continuum, my thoughts are that in organisational life, namely on Boards and in senior management teams, the likelihood is that our toxic humans will demonstrate *elements* of ASPD and psychopathic traits. If you recall Al Dunlap ('Chainsaw Al') from Chapter 1 and the recorded observation of him by others – and then glance through Table 1, a cursory listing of elements from what we know about Dunlap would make him a pretty toxic individual with behaviour suggestive of psychopathy:

- Being deceitful;

- Acting impulsively;

- Being irritable and aggressive;

- Being consistently irresponsible;

- Having a lack of remorse;

- Lacking empathy;

- Displaying arrogance;

- Lacking guilt;

- Displaying goal-oriented behaviour.

If Al was here, he would probably consider the last item – 'displaying goal-oriented behaviour' – to be a *plus* rather than a minus. This item

Table 1. Antisocial Personality Disorder (ASPD) and Psychopathy.

ASPD	Psychopathy
A person must display at least three of these items for a diagnosis of ASPD by a healthcare professional	Additional signs that a person may have psychopathy – additional to ASPD symptoms
• Disregarding the law	• Lack of empathy
• Being deceitful	• Arrogance
• Acting impulsively or being incapable of planning	• Charisma
• Being irritable and aggressive	• Excessive vanity
• Being consistently irresponsible	• Lack of guilt
• Having a lack of remorse	• Difficulty processing other people's facial expressions
	• Goal-oriented behaviour
	• Insensitivity to punishment

Source: Adapted from Smith Haghighi (2021).

suggests an approach to life which truly sees the means justifying the ends – winning at (almost) any cost. Al would likely maintain that 'acting impulsively' was a decisive leadership quality – even though he was guilty of making decisions on the hoof, i.e. without proper thought or preparation, often in a matter of seconds. Jon Ronson shares the following interaction with Al Dunlap about an employee he saw as lazy:

> *He [Dunlap] had a little gold axe on his lapel. As we ate, he told me funny stories about firing people. Each was essentially the same: someone was lazy and he fired them with an amusing quip. For instance, one lazy Sunbeam executive mentioned to him that he just bought himself a fabulous sports car.*
>
> *"You may have a fancy sports car," Al replied, "But I'll tell you what you don't have. A job!"*
>
> (Ronson, 2011 p. 167)

So in terms of what forms and builds a toxic human, I think we are starting to get a pretty good picture – albeit a general outline without the detail (yet) of all the active ingredients. What else needs to be added in?

Well, from the interviews that I've conducted with people who have been victims of or associated with toxic humans in organisations and on Boards, one of the biggest areas of interest is without doubt *narcissism*. So let's now take a look at how narcissism features as one of the major characteristics of toxic humans in the workplace.

NARCISSISM

I'm fairly sure if I asked you whether you had had experience of working with a narcissist, you would say yes. That narcissist might have been a coworker – or possibly worse – your boss. As human beings, we reckon we are quite adept at identifying who's a narcissist and who isn't. But as the saying goes, 'still waters run deep' and it's entirely possible for someone to be a narcissist or to have narcissistic traits but to be as quiet as a church mouse: someone who doesn't make an overt display of any of the classic narcissistic traits or behaviours such as:

- Unrealistic, grandiose self-image;

- Incredibly self-centered;

- Speak only about themselves;

- Feeling special and unique;

- Arrogance and haughtiness;

- Quick to criticise and judge others;

- Highly sensitive to criticism;

- Think the rules don't apply to them;

- Constant self-promotion;

- Feeling entitled to the best of everything;

- Value power and fame;

- Demand constant acknowledgement;

- Will respond with aggression when questioned;

- Deceitful and manipulative.

Source: Thomas Erikson, *Surrounded by Narcissists*, Penguin Random House, 2022.

An example of just how corrosive the behaviour of a narcissist can be relates to a story shared with me by a long-standing acquaintance who told me the story of one of the members of the senior management team in his company who persisted in parking his car in the front parking lot reserved for clients and guests – as opposed to parking at the rear of the building like everybody else. Despite constant remonstrations by my acquaintance – who was junior to this senior manager – about how everybody noticed that he parked his car in the front, and that this looked like he was breaking the rules, the senior manager ignored all representations with a retort that, as one of the *top* leaders in the organisation, he could park where he bloody well liked. The actual scatological language of the retort is not printable. Such behaviour is highly corrosive in the sense that it undermines the code of conduct that is supposed to be observed by all employees. If a senior manager is seen to be flagrantly flouting the rules, trust is compromised. And when the reaction to being challenged is so nasty (See 'Will respond with aggression when questioned' above), narcissists can be truly scary. So narcissistic behaviour, far from being just about a self-centered person, is in fact one of the more insidious sources of toxicity in organisations.

Occasionally, some narcissistic behaviour is as ridiculous as is terrifying. An old friend of mine, a highly successful executive, once told me about a meeting with a client that she attended with her female boss. The meeting went extremely well, and my friend felt elated by the experience. However, as both women climbed into the taxi after the meeting, the boss suddenly turned to her subordinate (my friend) with a ferocious look and said: '*Never* show up to a meeting again with me, with that (pointing at my friend's designer handbag) – have you any idea how embarrassing it was that you showed up with a bag like that? It made me look like the poor cousin! Never do that again, do you hear me!' Episodes like these are never forgotten by the victim – in stark contrast to the narcissistic perpetrator who could not care less, and who sails on through life leaving a trail of (very often) devastated people. The character Miranda in *The Devil Wears Prada* is a humorous example of an über-narcissist who berates her staff at every opportunity and when she's finished her tirade, dismisses them with a cursory wave of her hand: 'That's all'. We can laugh at her behaviour (after all, it's a movie), but such characters provide us with a valuable reminder that the world contains people like Miranda (and in fact, a lot, lot worse). As we will discover later, Boards are a favourite place for narcissists to gather. And once they have taken up residence, they are very difficult to dislodge.

BUT STILL, WHAT IS IT THAT CAUSES PEOPLE TO BE TOXIC HUMANS?

We will explore matters in more depth when we look at early childhood experiences later in the book (Chapter 7). What we know is that some people are genetically predisposed towards psychopathy or antisocial behaviour disorder, and that this can be exacerbated by the family environment as the person grows into an adult. So as far as we know now, it is a combination of nature and nurture. The important thing to bear in mind is that a person with certain traits associated with psychopathy is not necessarily going to turn into a criminal psychopath (although as we shall see, it does seem that senior leadership teams in organisations and Boards – have a much higher number of them, i.e. psychopaths). As Thomas Erikson shares:

> *Generally speaking, we could say that a psychopath is everything a narcissist is plus more. A psychopath is prepared to do anything to achieve their goals........*
>
> *Less intelligent psychopaths are often incarcerated. The criminal justice system in Sweden estimates that 25% of all prisoners in the country are clinical psychopaths. That alone is a good reason for anybody to stay well clear of prisons.*
>
> *For smarter psychopaths it's a very different story. Other popular data suggests that 10% of all people in upper managerial positions are psychopaths. This goes for all kinds of organisations, from drug cartels to religious movements. It's hard to verify this data but it's obvious that the higher up in an organisational hierarchy, the greater the ratio of psychopaths will be. The reason for this is simple: psychopaths crave power and attention. They believe that they belong at the top of the food chain, and that makes it only natural for them to seek to rise in the ranks. As is usually the case, they will utilise any acceptable means and a few more besides, to get what they want.*
>
> (Erikson, 2022)

The leadership guru Simon Sinek and the leadership academic Robert ('Bob') Sutton have both done a great job of drawing our attention to the existence of 'the jerk' (as Simon Sinek often calls the person, along with 'asshole') or 'the asshole' (the term Bob prefers to use). In Simon Sinek's YouTube video 'The Most Toxic Person In The Workplace' (2020), he maintains it is 'unbelievably easy to find the asshole on the team'. Everyone on the team can identify this person. Sinek uses the US Navy Seals as an example of an organisation that, like others, is looking for 'High Performance, High Trust' individuals (ones that have always 'got your back'). A 'High Performance, Low Trust' individual is what Sinek calls 'a toxic leader and a toxic team member'. You don't want such individuals on your team. What you would rather have are (of course) High Performers, High Trust or Medium Performance, High Trust or even Low

Performance, High Trust people on your team. So far so good: the key variable is trust. If, however, you introduce the element of psychopathy or antisocial behaviour disorder into the mix, then I believe it can become a whole lot harder to discern the asshole or the jerk on the team. We know that psychopaths or people with psychopathic tendencies are often charming people: they know how to manipulate others. And while most of the literature will say that these people eventually get found out (phew!) – the problem is the damage they cause up to and until they are caught out or called out. Take, for example, the bullying technique known as 'gaslighting'. Gaslighting is a term that describes how a bully identifies his victim and then slowly but surely starts the process of gradually undermining the professionalism of the person, casting doubt on their decision-making abilities and offering up 'supportive and helpful suggestions' that are really just ways of insinuating that the person has certain weaknesses of which they themselves are not aware and that only others around them can see. Gaslighting originates from a play by Patrick Hamilton produced in 1938 which was known as *Angel Street* in America and later became a film directed by Alfred Hitchcock (Gas Light). In the movie, the husband tries to make his wife believe that she is losing her mind by slowly but surely, without her knowledge, turning down the flame on a gas lamp and creating a gradual change in the ambience of their home. He intentionally manipulates her environment and encourages her to start believing that she has a problem discerning reality, fuelling a self-destructive paranoia. In a stage version of the play in London, in the prewar years before World War Two, the husband and his lover try to convince the man's wife that they can *smell* gas. Either way, whether it's turning down the gas lamp or saying that you can smell gas, the technique of gradually eroding someone's grasp of the here and now has become known as gaslighting. And it's a pervasive technique which doesn't observe national boundaries.

What we also see is that some toxic humans do not even bother themselves with the gaslighting technique before telling people what they think of them! In a conversation with Frances, who works in the international higher education sector and was involved in a global expansion project – which involved the upheaval of relocating from her home base halfway round the world to help build a new facility in a new country – Frances shared that one day, her toxic boss sat her down and without warning, said: 'You are very bad at your job and I want to send you back'. Unbelievable! And although her boss wasn't immediately able to kick her out, her openly dismissive and condescending attitude to Frances invited others on the team to jump into the fray and start bullying Frances – in other words, the boss gave her tacit approval for others to start taking Frances down. Frances attributes the possibility for this to happen to the toxic culture existing in her organisation – where such behaviour is never called out and condemned, but rather, it is systemically condoned. It is what I would term '**systemic toxic collusion**', and we will delve deeper into this in later chapters.

Before we move on to Chapter 3, where we will consider in detail the kind of effect toxic humans have at Board level, in senior teams and on the business or organisation, let us acknowledge Bob Sutton who I mentioned earlier – the author of the *No Assholes Rule*. He was one of the first people not only to shine a light on those individuals we are calling toxic humans in this book but to also call vociferously for action against these people. In an article in the *Harvard Business Review* ('Why I Wrote The No Asshole Rule: Building a Civilized Workplace and Surviving One That Isn't', HBR, 17 March 2007), Bob said:

> *I was determined to use the word ******* in the title because to me other words like "jerk", "bully", "tyrant", "despot" and so on are just euphemisms for what people really call those creeps.… I know the term offends some people but nothing else catches the emotional wallop.*

He went on to say, due to the reaction from some people to the word '*******':

> *Harvard Business School Assistant Professor Boris Grosberg wrote me that they called it the No ******* Rule at Lehman [Brothers], but he had to write it as the "No Jerk" rule in his teaching cases.……*

And I think the other major contribution that Bob made, showing Bob's prescience in these things, is:

> *There are things that people out there who are victims of bullies can do to fight back and* **the word needs to get out.**
>
> (Sutton, 2007)

The words in bold in that remark from Bob are rendered in bold by me: **the word needs to get out**. It is interesting that one of Lehman Brothers' practices back in 2007 or so was to have the No Jerk (or No Asshole) Rule in place to govern their selection and recruitment strategy. It's ironic that it was only a year after Bob mentioned them using the No Asshole Rule that Lehman Brothers collapsed in spectacular fashion when they filed for bankruptcy on 15 September 2008. It was the largest corporate bankruptcy filing in history, with their CEO Richard ('Dick') Fuld characterised as a charismatic but narcissistic leader. A year later, my friend Stefan Stern in the Financial Times (22 September 2009) wrote:

> One year on from the fall of Lehman Brothers, the face of Dick Fuld, former chief executive, has been back on our television screens. Some of his greatest hits have received another airing. "When I find a short seller*, I want to tear his heart out and eat it before his eyes while he's still alive," he declares in one clip.
>
> (Stern, 2009)

*a short seller is someone who bets on asset prices going down rather than up

I wonder if Fuld was aware of the No Asshole Rule at Lehman Brothers when he said this!

Fuld certainly meets our working litmus test of a toxic leader (someone who leaves an organisation worse off than when that person arrived there). 28,000 people lost their jobs, and that was just for starters when you consider the turmoil and anguish that resulted from the bankruptcy. If you watch a recording of Lehman Brothers Bankruptcy testimony (YouTube AmericanRhetoric.com, 7 January 2018), you will be able to observe Dick Fuld answering questions about his eye-wateringly high executive compensation as well as having to effectively agree that he played a significant role in deciding the composition of the Corporate Governance Committee which in turn had oversight of the Compensation Committee which in turn decided how much he would be paid as CEO. Judging by the frequency of his tongue-flicking tic while giving testimony, Fuld must have felt under intense pressure. But like the narcissistic behaviours we have looked at ('grandiose self-image'; 'arrogance and haughtiness'), Fuld still manages to keep his cool.

And after 1 hour and 59 minutes of questioning, you are left wondering: is Fuld going to apologise? The chair of the committee, Rep. Henry Waxman, then says in his concluding remarks: 'What I didn't hear from you Mr Fuld, [while] you said you took responsibility for the decisions you made: in retrospect you [did] say that you should have done things different [sic] but you don't seem to *acknowledge* that you did anything wrong... and that I think is also troubling to me.' Fuld is silent, at which point the committee hearing ends. Fuld stands up, impassive and leaves the room.

As we see with toxic humans, they are never wrong.

3

WHAT EFFECT DO TOXIC HUMANS HAVE AT BOARD LEVEL, IN SENIOR TEAMS AND ON THE BUSINESS OR ORGANISATION?

Let's begin our look at the effect of toxic humans in the boardroom, at senior levels and on the organisation as a whole by first defining what we think of when we talk about the toxic workplace:

> A toxic workplace refers to a **dysfunctional and stressful professional environment**. It could be that the people in charge are bullies, or the organisational culture is bent on winning regardless of what it takes. It could even be that coworkers are inconsiderate or even abusive. Whichever one it is, toxic workplaces can be detrimental to not just your physical and mental health but also to your happiness and your professional growth.
> (Professional Alternatives Staffing Solutions, 31 December 2021)

Members of Boards should in theory have a bird's eye view of what is going on in an organisation and be able to pick up evidence of toxicity in that organisation. Is it reasonable to expect this of them? Let's focus on Boards in this chapter and what they do, then we will touch on senior teams – and then return to board members again later on.

BOARDS TODAY

What are Boards like nowadays and what exactly do they do? Here's a view from *The Economist* on corporate Boards:

In the popular imagination, a corporate board seat looks like the cushiest sinecure in business. Board members appear to get paid – often handsomely – to attend a few meetings a year and to nod knowingly as the chief executive pontificates on strategy. They seldom make the news unless the occasional tut-tut results in the CEO being shown the door, or an activist investor campaigns for a seat at an iconic company (as has happened in recent months at Disney, Salesforce and Tesla). Once the errant boss is out or the activist campaign is over, either because it succeeded or, as in Disney's case, the challenger is placated with concessions, the board slinks back into comforting obscurity...

In fact, these low-key shareholder representatives have never been busier. *They are expected to help bosses navigate war, geopolitical strife, the return of high inflation, climate change and technological disruption, all in the aftermath of a once-in-a-century pandemic. [And] stricter corporate-governance rules have forced company directors to be more accountable.......*

[So] as a result, they are working harder and longer than before, often on top of their demanding day jobs as executives at other firms.

(The Economist, 2023)

It looks like – compared to 30 years ago – that the role of the board member has changed considerably. The same article notes:

Thirty years ago directors amounted to little more than window dressing, recalls Charles Elson, a boardroom veteran and corporate-governance expert at the University of Delaware. Management teams "basically ran the show", he says. Boards were stuffed with friends of the managers or of other board members. These days a self-respecting board ought to contain an expert on supply chains, the Federal Reserve, China, ESG, AI—the list goes on. Layer on top of that requirements for "diversity, equity and inclusion"—i.e., ensuring that not everyone is a white male—and cobbling together a board has become high-stakes corporate sudoku.

(The Economist, 2023)

The business of meeting and dealing with these challenges is one of the drivers behind the establishment of the Virtual Advisory Board (VAB) www.virtualadvisoryboard.co.uk, which is a global organisation set up to help talented individuals who are seeking their first Board position while at the same time, supporting organisations to strengthen and diversify their Board talent pool through helping them to expand their portfolio of expert board members. VAB recognises the need to enrich boards of directors and advisory boards with people from diverse backgrounds and expertise, while supporting the human aspect of being on a Board. VAB learning programmes aid members in understanding how best to interact effectively and compassionately with fellow board members who are different from one another. Such efforts are promising for improved Board performance and enhanced board member capabilities in the future.

MORE PROGRESS TO BE MADE

As *The Economist* article mentioned, past Boards were 'stuffed' with people's 'friends' – and there is plenty of evidence to suggest that such practices are far from over and that many Boards are still composed of cliques and cabals of people and their buddies. So against this backdrop of the changing nature of Boards today, some issues are being thrown into sharp relief. One of these continues to be the role of the Board in overseeing risks to the business – and I think it is important to state that these are not just obvious risks (like the effect of a new, competitive entrant into the organisation's sector or the need to comply with the environmental, social and governance (ESG) requirements that the organisation has signed up to) – there are in addition existential risks that are to do with the culture of the organisation – and as a consequence, risk around the ability to be able to continue to attract and retain critical talent. If your organisation becomes less and less of a talent magnet because of an erosion in the employer brand due to reputational damage (and, say, a cold or negative image), it may prove increasingly hard, given the resulting talent exodus, for the organisation to achieve its objectives.

CAN BOARDS DETECT TOXICITY?

Some of the signs of toxicity that Boards should be on the lookout for are more obvious than others. Board members interact with senior members of the organisation on a fairly regular basis and in general, they get to meet and talk occasionally with other more junior members of the organisation. Perceptive and empathetic board members will notice through the observation of human interactions within the organisation any instances of passive-aggressive behaviour from bosses (and also teammates). If they are allowed access to employee data from human resources, board members might also notice increasing rates of absenteeism – and they might hear anecdotally about any presenteeism (being present at your workplace longer than required, as a sign that the person is worried about losing their job) that might be occurring. Again, if workforce data is part of the regular reporting of an organisation, board members might also start to notice unusually high attrition rates which could include frequent turnover of the senior management and also, looking a bit deeper, within the middle manager demographic as well. More infrequently board members might also notice flashes of intimidation by senior members of the organisation of peers and reports – which could include an unnecessarily harsh tone of voice, bullying or public blaming, i.e. within board meetings, calling out certain employees for things that are going wrong or to justify key objectives that were not met. Board members who take the time to talk to individuals within the organisation might also get an intimation of other kinds of insidious behaviour or even gaslighting, although this might be harder to discern. A cursory glance at dates and times of emails sent by senior managers to other members of the organisation might also reveal to board members that emails are being sent out of hours and that the frequency of these emails might be quite astonishing. What board members might not be able to sense, without having some degree of empathy or a bit of detective work, at least in the period before things start to really unwind in the organisation, is a pervasive lack of care which results in what we might call the creation of a 'compassion- and empathy-free zone' within the organisation. Board members might start to notice trust issues surfacing or perhaps begin to get an overall feeling of a lack of trust developing that appears to be leading to a lack of psychological safety. It may be that board members notice the lack of psychological safety through a different route, such as a symptom of the stasis they detect around innovation and creativity within the organisation: new product development has stalled and the organisation seems to be stuck. Again, if the data is recorded and shared, the number of sick days taken by employees in a particular part of the organisation might be suggestive of the start of a localised mental ill health crisis within the organisation as the result of the actions or behaviour of a particular manager.

Perhaps most worrying of all, and this might not be so easy to see, is that the true *purpose* of the organisation is actually in terminal decline. Like the metaphorical boiling frog story (a frog in a pot of tepid water that gradually gets heated to boiling point won't notice the gradual change until it is too late), board members who have been around for a long time may not have picked up on the change until things have reached crisis level. And at that point, drastic action on the part of the Board is required to course correct.

THE CRITICAL IMPORTANCE OF PURPOSE

John Barker, VP Strategic Planning & Thought Leadership at the Bonar Institute, an advisory firm based in Ottawa, Canada, and itself a leading voice in purposeful leadership, is a great advocate for the importance of purpose in Boards, organisations and indeed, life. In my conversation with John, he shared the following:

- Self-awareness of board members at the *individual* level is vital;

- Then comes self-awareness at the *Board* level;

- Shared goals of board members at the *individual* level is key, too; and

- Then come shared goals of the Board *as a whole*.

John proposes that this all needs an 'on-going tune-up' given that the world is constantly changing. He advises organisations to go back to the basics and restate the importance of public purpose, something that John fears has been forgotten. Boards then need to address knowledge gaps, optimise skills, understand board member intentions for being on the Board, study the decision sciences and apply appropriate psychometrics to the Board as individuals and as a collective (more about this in Chapter 6) and last but not least, educate all stakeholders about the workings of the Board. John is passionate about the need for Boards to be innovative and in his role at the Bonar Institute, he also coaches Boards to think deeply about their decision-making capabilities, their curiosity and their ability to adapt.

EROSION OF TRUST – HOW DO BOARDS COME IN?

If we ponder the question of trust for a moment, and how to build trust in organisations, I believe the tone and behaviour of people in the organisation must be set from the top and this would include not just the CEO and her team, or senior managers in the organisation, but the Board of Directors itself. All these people must lead the way.

But what of dysfunctionality in Boards? In their book *Boards That Lead*, Ram Charan, Dennis Carey and Michael Useem point out the following:

> *In our experience, as many as half of Fortune 500 companies have one or two dysfunctional directors. Not infrequently, an intimidated management ends up kowtowing, fine-tuning its presentations in the boardroom to anticipate the difficult director's reactions or consulting with the director in time-consuming ways accorded to no others. It becomes a drain for everyone involved – except the dysfunctional director.*
>
> (Charan et al., 2014, p. 62)

They also qualify their remarks:

> *Let us be clear. We are not critical of directors who disagree with management strategy or voice alternative directions. We're not even talking about hostile directors sometimes forced onto the board by a hedge fund trying to take control of the company or about partisan factions that have formed for whatever reason…. Dysfunctional directors have their own modus operandi……[and] the result is to impair, even negate, a board's capacity to lead the firm. As in any group, a dysfunctional member can sabotage the entire team.*
>
> (Charan et al., 2014, p. 62)

Staying with the subject of trust, here's a perspective shared with me by one of my interviewees, a member of a senior management team with deep experience of interacting with the Board:

> *My expectation when I'm presenting at a board meeting is that we on the management team expect to get challenged: the directors have personal liability and when things break down between board and management it's always due to a lack of trust. As a member of management your life expectancy in the firm is based on what the board thinks of you. It's an unequal relationship because control is with the board. I've been in environments which are really nasty where people get smashed. The behaviour in the board is so extreme that if this happened in the organisation itself you would whistle blow and action would be taken. Before interacting with Boards myself, I didn't expect any of this. You don't get taught what to expect. And you don't know what to expect.*

> *[If things get bad] how do you whistle blow against your board when you have no protection? You have two options: one, you suck it up or two, you leave. There is no third option. I've seen grown men in their 50s coming out of board meetings crying. People can be eviscerated at these meetings. . . .*

> *I've also worked with boards where the members are extremely professional and supportive. I've noticed that board members who also have roles on other boards can very often bring in ideas and help to build value. You can feel confident to say to a board member: "Well, I'm thinking about this – what do you think?" and that's a good place to be.*

DYSFUNCTIONAL BOARDS – WHAT DOES IT TAKE TO CREATE THE PERFECT STORM?

So what people dynamics might be at play to create the conditions for a perfect storm, a worst-case scenario affecting the ability of a Board to be effective? What might be happening or what might we observe? What might a dysfunctional board member look like?

To help us think about these things, I have created a set of toxic personas. I call these the Six 'M' Toxic Board Personas.
These are:

1. The Monster,

2. The Mouse,

3. The Mouth,

4. The Moaner,

5. The Micromanager, and

6. The Muser.

Let's take a look at these personas individually and let's consider what kind of impact they have on interpersonal Board dynamics.

THE MONSTER

The Monster is best described as the archetypal narcissistic corporate psychopath. He – and it is usually a 'he' – is intent at control and domination at all costs. This person is often extremely charming and smooth. I also like to think of this person as being 'hubris personified', i.e. a person with excessive pride or confidence. They are able to put on a show of authentic 'active listening' complete with head nodding and murmuring of assent as they canvass for opinions, but in truth the Monster's mind is made up because he thinks his solution, without question, is the best. The Monster is very skilled at using 'corrupted empathy' for nefarious purposes. He knows how to get under the psychological skin of people, to discern their weaknesses and exploit them for his own ends. In summary, the Monster is a complete bully and the epitome of a Machiavellian personality, i.e. a manipulative personality. Delroy L. Paulhus and Kevin M Williams explored the Machiavellian personality alongside subclinical narcissism and subclinical psychopathy (which we addressed in Chapter 2) and concluded that:

....the Dark Triad of personalities [Narcissism, Machiavellianism and psychopathy], as currently measured, are overlapping but distinct constructs........[and] in non-clinical samples, members of the Dark Triad share a common core of disagreeableness.
(Paulhus & Williams, 2002)

Disagreeableness! Something to watch out for.

THE MOUSE

In complete contrast to the Monster, the Mouse stays quietly in the background. Secretly, the Mouse is anxious about being out of his depth and so decides to keep a low profile to avoid exposing either his lack of knowledge of the business/activities of the organisation or his inability to deal with complex or complicated issues. You might wonder how the Mouse manages to get onto the Board in the first place. Typical examples might be where you have a family-owned business and the Mouse is a member of the clan. They are there to represent the interests of the family, but with the passing of the decades the fire, energy and enthusiasm of the founders has more or less evaporated by the time the Mouse is on the team. The Chinese have a saying: 富不过三代 (*fù bù guò sān dài*) which literally translates as: Wealth does not pass three generations, i.e. wealth does not survive beyond three generations – and so for many companies in the part of the world where I live, where they are family-owned, this concern forms part of the background music to their lives – although of course no one really wants to talk about it. So for the Mouse, silence is by far the safest bet (sometimes, these family members are Musers too). And of course the Mouse is more than happy to acquiesce to the views of the stronger members of the Board (especially where there is a tyrannical Monster Chair). This tendency is seldom lost on the Monster who will use a combination of flattery and obsequiousness to invite the support of the Mouse in furthering the aims of the Monster.

THE MOUTH

The Mouth is never happier then when he is taking centre stage, talking voluminously and holding court. The Mouth has a tendency to be domineering and is completely lacking in self-awareness. Weaker Chairs of Boards find it a constant battle to grab airtime when they have the Mouth as part of their team. Of course, the situation is even worse if you have two or more Mouths on the same Board. The Mouth will even try to fill spaces in the conversation or discussion when in fact silence may be called for or could well be the best policy at that moment in time. The Mouth regards himself as a supremely valuable member of the team and considers himself a great listener, whereas in reality the Mouth is a terrible listener except when it comes to listening to his own voice.

THE MOANER

The Moaner is a fixture of most Boards unfortunately. The Moaner, in a misplaced belief that it is part of their role as a critical friend to the CEO and the senior management team to be relentlessly critical, never has a positive word to say about anything that the senior management team has done. The Moaner will typically lead the way to look at 10 things management has done and then focus on those two items in the list which are still a work in progress and which for very good reasons the team has not yet had a chance to address – and then to complain bitterly and persistently about them (The eight things that *have* been done well are all but ignored). Too often, the Moaner lacks the imagination and creativity to offer alternative views and when challenged or asked about what they would do differently, their retort is often 'That's not my job, that's yours.' The Moaner is your archetypal doom and gloom merchant.

THE MICROMANAGER

The Micromanager is a frustrated doer who truly believes (although they try to hide this) that they can run things better than management. The Micromanager is completely unable to get out of the weeds and elevate the discourse in order to take part in important strategic discussions about the future of the organisation. The Micromanager often has a tragically small worldview. Their weakness as a board member is that their perspectives are too granular and they lack the innovation and creativity to be able to see the bigger picture. Given that one of the roles of a Board is to manage risk, the Micromanager is often the one who causes the Board to take what they feel is a prudent or safe approach to a potential innovation where the thinking is that it is much better (=safer) to put the brakes on something, to stop it outright, than to take an informed, strategic, risk-factored decision.

THE MUSER

The Muser is the person who sits quietly listening to the goings-on of the Board – and you might be forgiven for thinking that the Muser is a Mouse. On closer examination, you might conclude that their silence is due to the fact that they are speculating about what might be on the menu for lunch. Unfortunately, what is often going on in their head is much more complicated and potentially disruptive, especially to the Chair of the Board who, if he or she is doing their job properly, is working hard to manage delicate egos and human dynamics within the Board and to navigate things such that the Board will be inclined to follow the guidance or direction from the Chair. This is why, when it comes, the sudden intervention by the Muser – which comes with little or no warning – can be the catalyst for chaos. When the Muser decides to speak up, their contribution is more often than not completely left-field, off-beam and off-topic: to call it a distraction for the Chair and the rest of the Board is an understatement. The Chair has to analyse in a nanosecond whether this intervention is paving the way to what could be the start of an alternative agenda to their own or whether it is just a moment of madness. Often it can be hard to tell. And, of course, I think it's fair to say that *well-intentioned* interventions by board members to bring the members of the Board to their senses, or to offer up a viable alternative solution, are always to be welcomed. The point is though that such interventions should be driven by concern for the organisation rather than allowing an individual member, in this case the Muser, the opportunity for self-aggrandisement (they are aware that they are 'taking power' away from the Chair, and they enjoy that moment). It is not about a flash of inspiration, a true 'a-ha' moment of realisation about something. For some skilful Musers, it's the self-aggrandisement that they're interested in and the delight they take in stirring things up, rather than truly wanting to offer up something valuable.

A WORD ABOUT THE CHAIR

It almost goes without saying that if the Chair has any of the characteristics of the Six 'M' Toxic Board Personas, the Board is in for any interesting ride!

I have shared these personas during a number of presentations and talks to people who are active members of Boards. We've had a lot of fun discussing them, not least because people have shared enthusiastically that they have a Moaner on their Board right now, or that they recognise some of the behaviours described, in themselves! My purpose in creating these personas was really to trigger a conversation about the nature and quality of discourse within Boards. We could probably apply the same set of personas to examine and reflect on the people dynamics within senior teams too.

In her ground-breaking book about Boards, *The Black Box of Governance*, Sandra Guerra also mentions certain archetypes which I share here as another datapoint for understanding the different personalities on Boards. This typology was developed by Richard Leblanc and James Gillies in their book, *Inside the Boardroom: How boards really work and the coming revolution in corporate governance* and cited in Sandra Guerra's book on boards:

Types of Dysfunctional Board Directors

'Caretaker' chairs – are unable to effectively run board meetings, do not deal with interpersonal conflicts and disagreements and do not relate well with the other directors, the CEO and the executive team. They should be replaced if they do not improve.

'Controllers' – dominate the functioning of the Board by competence, diplomacy, humour or anger. They are very dangerous, especially when the Board includes dysfunctional directors who are unable to neutralise them.

'Conformists' – are board directors who do not collaborate and do not perform, who support the status quo and are rarely prepared for any serious discussion. They tend to be liked on account of past successes or relationships and may have been CEOs or politicians who now enjoy limited credibility.

'Cheerleaders' – are 'enthusiastic amateurs' who constantly praise the directors, the CEO and the executive team, but are unprepared for meetings, heedless of the strategic issues faced by the company and usually ask stupid questions. At worst, they are viewed with contempt, at best, they are known as 'sleepers', 'non-performers' or 'ineffective'.

'Critics' – are constantly criticising and complaining in an aggressive tone of voice and with harsh words. The other board directors refer to them as 'manipulative' or 'sneaky'. In addition, they lack the ability to dissent in a constructive way, which is a characteristic of challengers or change agents.

Source: Sandra Guerra (2021, p. 197)

The identification of the 'caretaker' Chair is a most valuable contribution to the formulation of these archetypes. And overall, such archetypes help us to understand the potential types of people we might encounter on the board and in so doing, helps us to start thinking about our strategy for working with them.

THE IMPORTANCE OF SELF-REFLECTION BY BOARDS

As I outlined in the introduction to *Toxic Humans*, I believe that self-reflection on the part of Boards is in general something that we need a lot more of. One of the reasons for this is that traditionally, board members and Board composition were never subjected to the kind of scrutiny that is normal procedure for when one is putting together a senior management team. Boards are now being thrust under the spotlight more than ever. And around the world, great work is being done by a number of organisations and individuals who recognise that Boards and their performance could be significantly enhanced if they were supported and helped. One of the ongoing difficulties for anyone wanting to research the dynamics of a Board is that they are by definition something of a 'closed book' and this accounts for the relative paucity of academic work on Boards (although there have been some excellent exceptions).

TOWARDS 'ROBUST, EFFECTIVE, SOCIAL SYSTEMS'

It is a sobering thought that such issues and questions (around the quality and performance of Boards) have been around for a long time. Jeffrey A. Sonnenfeld of Yale School of Management wrote in the Harvard Business Review back in 2002 that:

> ...if following good governance regulatory recipes doesn't produce good boards, what does? The key isn't structural, it's social. The most involved, diligent, value adding boards may or may not follow every recommendation in the good governance handbook. What distinguishes exemplary boards is that they are robust, effective social systems.
>
> (Sonnenfeld, 2002)

Professor Sonnenfeld was really on to something here. Transparency and good governance should be 'givens' for a Board and how it behaves. Much harder to achieve is excellence in teamwork, often because of the dominance of certain types of people on Boards. I think most people would agree that to enable Boards to be truly effective, there must be capacity within the Board to have and to manage constructive disagreement. I do not believe that anyone would say that achieving absolute harmony is what we are after: but what we *are* after are Boards that are more empathetic and mutually supportive than we have seen in the past – 'robust, effective social systems' as Professor Sonnenfeld outlined more than 20 years ago. What we need are Boards that are cohesive, consisting of proper grown-ups – rather than what people more often get, which is a toxic, motley crew of towering egos all jostling for supremacy.

BUT WHY SHOULD ALL THIS MATTER?

Duke Haddad, writing in NonProfit Pro, frames the issues brilliantly when he quotes an article from *The Houston Chronicle* ('The Chron'):

> *The Chron notes that a dysfunctional board of directors can damage an organization internally and potentially cause external negative publicity. A board in a dysfunctional state shows a lack of confidentiality, conflicting agendas, lack of order, lack of respect for others, promotes a hostile environment, creates secret meetings, fosters personal agendas, has a lack of trust, and creates an environment of dominating members plus non-participating members. This type of board if left unchecked could dramatically affect staff leadership and organizational direction.*
>
> (Haddad, 2022)

We can see how the effect of board members displaying the toxic behaviour of the Six 'M' personas could contribute to the creation of all of the issues listed by Duke Haddad. The Chron goes further and enumerates what it calls the *Top Ten Signs of a Dysfunctional Board of Directors*. I have rendered these in a table form and added the Six 'M' persona types to illustrate who might be the main cause of the issue in question, or who might be contributing to the chaos (I have also added in the Chair as the lynchpin person):

Table 2. The Top 10 Signs of a Dysfunctional Board and the Source of the Toxicity.

	Issue	Important Considerations	Source of Toxicity
1	Lack of confidentiality	Board members must be on the same page as the head of the organisation	The Mouth – by being indiscreet
2	Conflicting agendas	If board members have conflicting agendas, it will be impossible to make decisions. They must all be on the same page.	The Muser – by introducing unhelpful and distracting topics
3	Lack of order	If board members jump from topic to topic and fail to discuss the most important matters at hand, they will be failing the organisation	The Chair – through an inability to manage and control the Board and its meetings

Table 2. (Continued)

Issue	Important Considerations	Source of Toxicity
4 Lack of respect	Board members must respect the CEO and vice-versa. Long-standing board members and new CEOs often display a pattern of mutual lack of respect	The Monster, the Mouse, the Micromanager – all are capable of taking umbrage for different reasons
5 Hostile environment	Some board meetings turn into opportunities for personal attacks rather than focusing on the business	The Monster, the Mouth, the Moaner – all are highly opinionated in various ways
6 Secret meetings	Separate or secret meetings are very destructive to the safe and effective functioning of the Board	The Chair, the Mouse – this may be the Chair's way of containing or managing legacy cliques – always messy. The Mouse may want to air his private views offline because of his 'emotional' connect with the business
7 Personal and political agendas	These agendas create a fog around decision-making and can render the Board impotent	All Six 'M's but potentially, the Monster most of all
8 Lack of trust	If the Board is not a model of trust, this poison will seep into the organisation itself and affect employees – with dire results	The Chair and all the board members through trust erosion (lack of credibility, lack of reliability, lack of human skills and rampant self-orientation)
9 Dominating members	Board members who are unable to work as a team and who talk too loudly or shut people down	The Monster, the Moaner, the Mouth – all are experts in this area – especially if they have narcissistic or psychopathic behavioural tendencies
10 Non-participants	Some board members are there solely because of the prestige it bestows on them and seldom offer opinions or ask questions	The Mouse – happy to be part of the meeting because it is an interesting day out and there is probably a nice meal or refreshments on offer

Source: Adapted from Stacy Zeiger (2023), and adapted with the Six 'M's personas by Michael Jenkins.

It is fairly clear from a quick glance at the table above that the Chair owns the major responsibility for the successful functioning of the Board. And connected to this is another piece: the nature and quality of the Chair's relationship with the CEO. Several years ago, I attempted to create an executive education programme in partnership with one of the United Kingdom's leading institutions for corporate governance in not-for-profit Boards where our aim was to bring the Chair and the CEO as a pair onto the programme, with an invitation to them (within a safe space) to explore their interpersonal dynamics and start the process of co-creating a better way of working together for the benefit of the organisation – and of course for their own well-being and success. Despite our best efforts and the interest we garnered from for-profit and not-for-profit organisations alike about this radical, human-centric programme, when it came to the crunch and we asked people to sign up as a pair, the realisation that the programme would tap into their vulnerabilities and require them to be very disclosing of their approach and thinking, people got anxious and skittish: before long, the initiative simply began to look like a bridge too far and we were unable to make it happen. The 'ask' was too great.

Other researcher/facilitators have had more luck in exploring board-management dynamics. In their fascinating study, 'Challenge in the boardroom: Director-manager question and answer interactions at board meetings', Helen R. Pernelet and Niamh M. Brennan were able to look at three NHS (UK National Health Service) Boards to try to understand how 'Non-Executive Directors (NEDs) challenge, question and dissent during board meetings'. They observed, audio-recorded and video-recorded the three Boards during nine board meetings. Given that it is NHS practice to have board meetings conducted in private and in public, their study can be considered truly unique. Some of their key findings were as follows:

- NEDs may be reluctant to offer moderate (i.e. constructive) challenge in public.

- There were significant differences between the level of dissent and the types of answers offered in public versus private (maybe not so surprising!).

- There is an association between the type of question asked and the type of answer given (NEDs often asked closed questions which triggered a yes/no response which tended to shut down further exploration of the area or issue being asked about).

The research team's empirical findings also suggest that Board behaviour 'varies in the presence of an audience of stakeholders'. Again, maybe not hugely surprising but for me, this raises interesting questions about the nature of trust and how it is created (or destroyed). The team also references a PricewaterhouseCoopers (PwC) 2019 report called 'The Collegiality Conundrum' where 43% of directors reported difficulty 'voicing dissent'. In a subsequent 2020 survey by PwC:

- 36% of directors said it was 'hard to voice a dissenting opinion' in their boardroom;

- 52% of directors reported that the desire to maintain collegiality contributed to 'muffled dissent' and

- 32% suggested this (difficulty in voicing dissent/maintaining collegiality) was due to 'dominant boardroom personalities'.

> PwC: Turning crisis into opportunity, PwC's annual corporate directors' survey, PwC Governance Insights Center (2020)

"Dominant boardroom personalities" – (the italics are mine) – well, it looks like the Monsters, Moaners and Mouths have made their mark!

Why is the issue of dysfunctionality and toxicity so critical? In the case of the United Kingdom's NHS, the Regulators introduced a requirement for NHS Boards to meet in public, in the interests of transparency and accountability, and enhanced communication about – and sharing of – what takes place in the NHS. What the researchers found was that challenge was milder in the public settings – a finding that suggests that the decision to conduct these meetings in public in order to improve matters – might not in reality have been validated. What I take from this is that Boards, like many teams, struggle to get the right amount of 'challenge' and 'support'. And if toxic humans and concomitant dysfunctionality are allowed to creep in and take hold, then things will quickly deteriorate and, as we have heard (and maybe you have experienced it yourself at first hand!) the organisation as a whole will suffer. This is why I am asserting that it is not just CEOs and their senior managers who need support and development – Boards do too (and urgently).

FOR WHAT THEN SHOULD WE BE AIMING?

In the preceding pages, I have tried to paint a picture of the dysfunctional personalities who can cause Boards to fail to perform as they should. We have enumerated some concrete examples of the forces that can derail Boards. If Boards were populated by more empathetic individuals, namely people who are capable of cognitive if not emotional or affective empathy (let's not get ahead of ourselves!) and who thereby are able to achieve that delicate balance of challenge and support, what kind of positive outcomes might we expect? In other words, what might be the effect of having *non-toxic* humans on the Board?

I think we can take inspiration from a number of organisations that are trying to improve how Boards work. Earlier in this chapter, I mentioned the VAB and the work that they do. In addition there is also the UK-based Leading Governance organisation. Leading Governance suggests that the following things are achievable if the right kind of approach is taken – and as you glance over it you will see that, like the earlier *Top Ten Signs of a Dysfunctional Board*, here we have 10 things the Leading Governance team feels are essential for Boards to be inspiring and well-led:

TEN THINGS THAT MAKE A GREAT BOARD

1. Understand their role and responsibilities;

2. Lead, not manage;

3. Engage with others;

4. Provide strategic, rather than operational support;

5. Have regular Board turnover and great succession planning;

6. Commit to ongoing learning and development;

7. Get the right information at board meetings;

8. Work as a team;

9. Challenge appropriately; and

10. Review their own performance.

For all of these things to happen and to work well, calling out toxicity and holding oneself to high standards seems to me to be a prerequisite. Current leadership thinking focuses a great deal on trust and psychological safety within an organisation. We should expect the same for Boards too. Furthermore, I have stressed the need to balance the right kind of challenge with the right kind of support and I think that's where non-toxic humans can *really* make a huge and positive impact. If we can enable this to happen, then the prize is the creation of an ecosystem that is resistant to toxicity and is able to create the right kind of conditions within which human beings can thrive and grow.

In 2017, Professor Andrew Kakabadse and his research team at Henley Business School, University of Reading produced a paper called 'Conflict and Tension in the Boardroom: How managing disagreement improves Board dynamics' in collaboration with ICSA, The Governance Institute wherein they note:

> *Each board member brings their own expertise, roles, responsibilities, goals and agendas. They may even take pride in their own levels of independence and objectivity. Despite these attributes, they must ultimately work as part of a wider team that is responsible for the organisation's long term interests. As such, **effective boards should be places of harmony and collaboration as well as challenge and independence.** Boards ideally act as environments in which each individual member can respect and incorporate the views of others and, when necessary, retain their independence and challenge fundamental assumptions.*
>
> (Kakabadse et al., 2017)

For Boards to truly become places of harmony and collaboration as well as of challenge and independence, we will need an overarching approach to combatting poisonous leadership in Boards.

In this chapter, we have explored the 'What?' of toxicity in boards today, and in Chapters 5 and 6, we will delve deeper to produce an actionable plan – 'Now What?'

4

SO WHAT DOES 'TOXIC HUMAN BEHAVIOUR' LOOK LIKE IN REAL WORKPLACE LIFE?

In this chapter, we will make a start on looking at what constitutes toxic human behaviour in the workplace and continue our investigation in subsequent chapters.

In conversations with different people, I asked what a toxic workplace means to them. Here are some comments to set the stage for this chapter.

WHAT DOES A TOXIC WORKPLACE LOOK LIKE TO YOU?

A toxic workplace for me means negativity, bullying and the feeling of being put down by people. You wake up in the morning and absolutely dread going to work. In my experience of a toxic workplace, it killed my enthusiasm for the work and turned me into a robot. It sapped my energy and confidence. The toxic workplace affects you out of work as well. It's like a negative emotion that's always there, it just sucks.

(International education specialist)

Toxicity in the workplace for me denotes someone, or a group of people, who creates a bad culture based on lies, dishonesty and narcissism. In my experience lots of leaders display these behaviours. I worked for a toxic boss with a great vision, but he put "Yes" people all around him and bought people off with presents. Once he suggested that I buy a new suit and shirt for myself, put these purchases on my expenses claim and then he would sign it off. I experienced him as very manipulative and he made me feel extremely uncomfortable.

(Management consultant)

Toxicity in the workplace – it's about certain personality types that are inappropriate on a number of levels; passive-aggressive, narcissistic, unreasonable, unfair, uncaring. It's a wide spectrum really, and when you're subjected to it, it makes your life miserable, stops you doing what you want to do, leaves you depleted. Then if they [toxic individuals] deal with you in a degrading manner as well, there is no ounce of anything that they have that could support you; they're not alive to anything that might matter to you and if they give you any credit, it is around something that satisfies their needs and does not recognise anything you believe you have done or your value contribution. That's toxicity. Not good.

(Coach and facilitator)

From the many conversations I have had with different people about the nature of toxic workplaces, my sense is that toxicity in organisations exists on a continuum: in other words – and perhaps not surprisingly – toxicity comes in varying degrees of intensity. In terms of getting an idea of what this continuum might look like, I have taken the amazing and highly perceptive work of the psychologist and scholar, Simon Baron Cohen, as a starting point for the concept of an 'Empathy-Toxicity Spectrum'. Baron Cohen is the author of a number of publications including *The Science of Evil* which is an examination of the nature of evil framed as a lack of empathy occurring in varying degrees and with different layers of complexity. Table 3 shows Baron Cohen's set of six levels of empathy starting with Level 0 (where the person has no empathy at all) to Level 6 which is where you find people who are exceptionally empathetic. I was particularly taken by Baron Cohen's thinking around the fundamental meaning of the word 'evil', given that 'evil' covers a wide range of things. As a word, according to Baron Cohen and paraphrased here, 'evil' does not really give us the level of granularity to be able to fully understand the *degree* of evil evident in a particular person or how exactly we might describe a heinous act. So, looking at 'evil' through the prism of 'levels of empathy' allows us to leverage a wide variety of data-driven insights from psychological surveys of people and their personalities and psychiatric research which in turn enables us to identify just how empathetic or lacking in empathy a person is. Of course, we do know that in the case of psychopaths, eliciting responses around what they think or feel about something is always going to be a challenge, given the typical behaviour of psychopaths which is to lie and obfuscate. This is why tests such as Robert Hare's Psychopath Test (the PCL-R) can help zero in on psychopathic traits that enable an accurate picture of an individual on a psychopathy scale even if we cannot elicit anything conclusive from an actual conversation with that person.

EMPATHY AND EVIL: UNDERSTANDING SIMON BARON-COHEN'S ANALYSIS OF EMPATHY AS A WAY TO UNDERSTAND EVIL

Baron-Cohen gives us a new way of looking at and defining what is going on for people by taking empathy as the starting point for analysing the inner workings of humans. It helps us to see why some people can empathise in a cognitive sense but not in an emotional (sometimes called 'affective') sense. Some people are unable to do either. It also helps us to see that depending on the case, the response required from the rest of us should be one that is based on compassion and an understanding of a person's unique situation, rather than a punitive response.

As Baron-Cohen states:

> ...*environmental triggers interact with our genetic predispositions and scientists are starting to discover particular genes that in far-reaching ways influence our empathy.... These are not genes for empathy per se but are genes for proteins expressed in the brain that – through many steps – are linked to empathy. These steps are still to be clarified, but we can already see from statistical analyses that genes exist that are associated with empathy.*
>
> (Baron-Cohen, 2011, with a new Foreword 2022)

A TOXICITY EQUATION

Baron-Cohen's insights are valuable as they give us the basis for creating a conceptual equation:

The Toxicity Equation©:

Toxicity in Humans at Work = Genetic Predisposition + Environmental Shaping* - Empathy + Work Context + Systemic Collusion

*childhood upbringing

We will revisit this Toxicity Equation© in subsequent chapters.

AN EMPATHY-TOXICITY SPECTRUM

In addition to the Toxicity Equation, I have also created a kind of 'Empathy-Toxicity Spectrum©' by developing a table-based summary of the key characteristics of the different levels of empathy (as shared by Baron Cohen in his book) and then mapping different degrees of toxicity onto it. I have then placed a box around those levels on the Spectrum (a 'continuum') which I believe are of greatest concern to us in the context of leaders and leadership in an organisational setting.

REFLECTIONS ON THE 'EMPATHY-TOXICITY SPECTRUM'

My intention in creating this table is to set the stage for reflection and discussion. So let's take a look at the different levels and what they might mean to us in terms of our interactions with people at work. It is important to bear in mind that the type of empathy we are noticing here is primarily affective or emotional empathy (as you will recall, we noted earlier that some people with strong psychopathic tendencies *can* empathise, i.e. they can see what their victims see in a *cognitive* sense and use that perceptive ability to take advantage of, harm or even destroy that person. But they are unable to achieve affective empathy).

Table 3. Empathy-Toxicity Spectrum.

LEVEL 0	LEVEL 1	LEVEL 2	LEVEL 3	LEVEL 4	LEVEL 5	LEVEL 6
No empathy at all	Still capable of hurting people	Major difficulties with empathy	Know they have trouble empathising	Slightly blunted empathy	Marginally above average in empathy	Remarkable level of empathy
Capable of committing serious crimes	Can reflect on what they have done	After shouting or saying hurtful things can realise they did wrong	May try to mask or compensate; avoid jobs which require demands on empathy	More comfortable with topics that do not touch on emotion	More women than men are at this level	Continually focused on other people's feelings
Hurting someone else means nothing	Cannot stop themselves at the point of hurting	Blunder through life saying all the wrong things	Find it hard to understand jokes or read facial expressions	Prefer having something practical to tackle	Careful about interactions at work and home but feelings not always on their radar	Go out of their way to check in and be supportive: people are never off their radar
Cannot experience remorse	Report that they 'see red'	Get in trouble for these 'faux pas'	Small talk and chatting is a nightmare	Friendships based on shared activities	Hold back from asserting opinions to avoid dominating	Tone of voice responses are enough to allow accurate assessment of someone's mood
Cannot understand what the other person is feeling	See victim as something to be destroyed or removed	Always mystified as to what they did wrong	Prefer to be alone at home 'to be themselves'	Avoid situations requiring emotional intimacy	Take their time to find out what is on another person's mind	An unstoppable drive to empathise with people
EXTREMELY TOXIC	HIGHLY TOXIC	TOXIC	IN-BETWEEN	NOT TOXIC	NON-TOXIC	HIGHLY NON-TOXIC

Source: Based on the work of Simon Baron-Cohen *(The Science of Evil, 2022)* and adapted by Michael Jenkins to suggest toxicity levels.

Level 0

I think most of us would be horrified at the thought of a Level 0 leader being the Chair of our Board or indeed the CEO leading our organisation! And yet it is possible. There are certainly many examples of Level 0 leaders in the world of politics – not just historical figures but contemporary ones as well. Experts in the field of psychiatry and the treatment of individuals with antisocial behaviour disorder (ASBD) are divided on whether it is possible to do anything substantive about people at Level 0 where they have committed terrible crimes – other than to protect them from themselves and society at large – which usually means incarceration for varying lengths of time if not whole life. Some criminal psychopaths – those who have raped and murdered people – are just too dangerous to ever be allowed out of prison or secure psychiatric facilities. It is hard to envisage any possibility of rehabilitation for such individuals. Then of course it is possible for us to encounter psychopaths who have not committed any crimes. My sense is that these people are more likely to be found at Level 1.

Level 1

At Level 1, we encounter people who are able to reflect on what they have done (in the aftermath of hurting someone – reflecting on how unacceptable it is but not being able to 'feel sorry' for the people they hurt): these individuals are likely to be impulsive and capable of doing great harm in a moment of abject rage – the classic 'red mist' that some people describe. They are calculating individuals who see people as objects, not human beings. This element of unpredictability makes people at Level 1 particularly dangerous. I think it is entirely possible to find people like this in corporate life – however, that element of 'lack of control' must thankfully limit the potential for such individuals to get into positions of influence and power.

Level 2

People at Level 2 will come across as cold and unfeeling – they have huge challenges when it comes to being able to empathise (affective or emotional empathy).

They are capable of realising that behaviour such as shouting or berating someone is highly undesirable, but unfortunately, they are unlikely to feel any remorse about what they have done. They might offer an abject apology which, combined with charm, might come across as genuine and true. But it is highly unlikely to be so. It is likely that a range of other conditions and mental disorders are also at play (especially when you read that such people 'blunder through life saying all the wrong things') in which case we might do well to approach them with compassion. Level 2 people are often trapped by their condition whereby they simply cannot fathom what it is they did that was (in many cases) so wrong. I think it is entirely possible for us to meet Level 2 people in organisational life – although with these kinds of hard-wired interpersonal impairments, one might wonder how long they might last, existing in a structure that has codes for acceptable conduct and which will eject people who contravene them.

Level 3

I am suggesting that people at Level 3 are borderline or 'in-between' in terms of their ability or otherwise – to empathise. Their cognitive empathy could well be second to none – whereas they will struggle with affective empathy. As you read in the list of observations that Level 3 type people find it hard to understand jokes or read facial expressions, it might be that their 'toxicity' – as experienced by co-workers – is something we could think about (1) tolerating/learning to live with and/or (2) trying to help them to manage. A number of the characteristics of Level 3 people contained in the table are highly suggestive of introverted – even painfully introverted – individuals. Their hesitancy around engaging in what they would see as pointless chit chat is an aspect that we might try to work through with them, encouraging them to see this as a very normal part of ordinary human interaction (especially in a work context) and giving them strategies to deal with their reticence and anxiety. There are also some people (roughly 10% of the general population) who have a condition known as alexithymia – which makes it difficult or impossible for them to 'name' their feelings. Alexithymia is the subclinical inability to identify and describe emotions experienced by one's self or others and is more prevalent in people on the autism spectrum. (Importantly, it is alexithymia that causes a lack of empathy in people with autism, not the autism itself). The core characteristics of alexithymia are marked dysfunction in emotional awareness, social attachment and interpersonal relating:

- Alexithymia isn't well understood. There's a possibility it may be genetic.

- The condition may also be a result of brain damage to the insula.

- This part of the brain is known for its role in social skills, empathy and emotions.

- It often coincides with another underlying neurological condition or mental health disorder. And while not inherently dangerous, this condition may inadvertently lead to *interpersonal and relationship issues*. It is possible that individuals with alexithymia are not only utilitarian in their judgments regarding moral issues and harm but also in their attitudes towards altruistic behaviour.

- They may be less aware of the emotions that typically encourage positive altruistic attitudes and *engage in a more deliberative and conservative cost-benefit analysis*.

Source: Anterior insula lesions and alexithymia reduce the endorsements of everyday altruistic attitudes - by Aileen Chau, Wanting Zhong, Barry Gordon, Frank Krueger, Jordan Grafman, in *Neuropsychologia* published by Elsevier.

It is clearly important, therefore, to consider a range of different elements when it comes to using the term 'toxic human': I think we would all agree that there are many things at play that we need to factor in.

Level 4

Over the past 25 years or so, I have had the opportunity to work with leaders at different levels and in many different sectors. Many of these leaders have risen to positions of power and authority by virtue of their excellent technical skills as – for example – engineers, lawyers or clinicians. During their rise to the top, these leaders may have had little or no opportunity to explore their expertise *as humans* or to reflect on their repertoire of leadership skills (including empathy and compassion). These leaders often encounter challenges when they suddenly find themselves leading a team – a massive change compared to the period in their careers when they were sole contributors without any management responsibilities – or when they were a junior member of a team. The challenge is exacerbated when an organisation is unable either through resource constraints or mindset – to support the development of these technically skilled but emotionally underdeveloped people. Level 4 is where many of these people are located. All this might sound a little bleak; however, with the right kind of development and support, these technically gifted employees can make the transition to become exemplars of excellent leadership. It's all a question of strategic planning and investment – and believing in and supporting organisational values around people development. Without specialist support to help exercise the empathy muscle (and to convey clearly that being empathetic and compassionate is *not* about being nice – it's about being fair and consistent), Level 4 people are likely to stay where they are: avoiding discussion of emotions and feelings; sticking to technical topics; staying resolutely in their comfort zone and saddest of all, generally missing out on the opportunity afforded by greater empathy skills to establish different types of friendships with more diverse groups of people. An inability for such leaders to progress *does matter*: employee expectations are rising around what they want their senior leaders to stand for, and there is a desire among Gen Z-ers for their leaders to be role models for a different, more progressive style of leadership. If an organisation is unable to facilitate this human skills 'dial-up', then it will lose out on critical talent and find its strategic aspirations stymied.

Level 5

People in this area are likely to be fairly reserved individuals who have the potential to strengthen their empathy (if they want to!) These are non-toxic people providing valuable service to their organisations, and they are comparatively self-aware – although they will benefit from feedback from a close colleague or friend about how they 'show up'. Level 5 leaders may also be interested in how they can improve their empathy. One way that they can do this is to think about how to become more *curious* about people and things – because there is an interesting link between being curious and having empathy. Curious people will be keen to ask their interlocutor about *their* life and the way *they* see things – so it's all about being intentional to focus the conversation around the other person rather than to talk about yourself straight away, or about what you think. As with everything, there is a happy balance to be struck: if in your enthusiasm to ask questions of the other person, the conversation begins to take on the tone of an interrogation or cross-examination, you might inadvertently cause the other person to shut down! So clearly, in this situation – when you see the other person looking around for an escape route – you would need to be conscious of that and of the need to tone things down! Other ways to increase your curiosity/empathy capability include reading widely and reading lots of different kinds of things – listening to podcasts and watching video clips of interesting and thought-provoking things. Reading poetry written by someone from a culture very different to yours can be a great way to gain new perspectives and new insights – both things that help us to strengthen our empathy. And of course there is growing recognition that special training (in leadership and management) can also target the development of a more empathetic approach.

Rebecca Knight writing in Insider magazine has this to share:

> *The best managers are those who see their employees not as vessels for accomplishing tasks but as people with families, responsibilities, and full lives outside work, according to Dane Jensen, a leadership expert who teaches at the Smith School of Business at Queen's University in Canada. So why are so many frontline managers still failing to do that? There are a few reasons, according to Mo Cayer, a professor of industrial and organisational psychology at the University of New Haven. But it often boils down to empathy fatigue. In Cayer's view, the problem is systemic.*
>
> *Fortunately, a vast body of research has found that empathic behaviours can be learned, and organisations should invest in leadership training and development.*
>
> (Knight, 2023)

Level 6

Level 6 is where we find people who are truly empathetic. In some ways, we can think of empathy as a kind of gift that these people have. At the same time, we will also find people who have thought very deeply and intentionally about how to behave in a more empathetic way – I'm thinking here, for example, about professional coaches and counsellors who have spent many years studying the art and science of the coaching and counselling processes – and who have spent a lot of time reflecting on people, how they behave and how they react to different situations. At this level, we are also likely to be entering the domain of what we call the 'Super Empaths'. These are people who are so empathetic they can find it almost overwhelming to be in certain situations that require an empathetic response – for example, they can be having conversations where they literally start to *feel and experience* the pain or anguish of the person with whom they are empathising. It is estimated that around 1–2% percent of the global population could be thought of as being 'Super Empaths'. So that's actually a lot of Super Empaths!

Crystal Jackson has written an excellent guide to being a Super Empath, and among the many things she points out, the following insights are particularly useful to know if you are trying to tackle toxicity in your life – and you are a Super Empath:

> *You're unlikely to tolerate toxic relationships because you don't have room for drama in your life. You want peaceful relationships that feel good and healthy to you... the difficult truth is that super empaths feel so much and so deeply that they often lose themselves - particularly in relationships.... [Super Empaths] can be so hyper-focused on taking care of everyone else that they forget to take care of themselves.*
>
> (Jackson, 2023)

From this, we can surmise that as with many things, too much of some-thing inherently positive can turn out in some cases to be challenging and problematic. The goal for managers is to strike the right balance of being empathetic and avoiding going to extremes, the reason being that as human beings, there is only so much that we can bear. The thing we're referring to now is what is known in compassion research and psychologically as 'distress tolerance', in other words an individual's ability to manage their internal emotional state in response to stress-inducing factors. The key is to take care of yourself so that you can do a good job of caring for others.

A WORD ON TOXIC LEADERS – MANAGING TO STAY ON AND STAY IN CHARGE

It is amazing how many toxic leaders manage to stay in charge long after passing their 'sell-by-date'. But through guile, luck in some cases, and what we might term 'systemic toxic collusion', many toxic leaders are able to cling on. Sometimes though, the Board finally takes notice – and takes action.

The Board Steps in to Remove the Toxic CEO

There have been cases where the Board has stepped in to remove the 'Toxic CEO'. It happened to Travis Kalanick at Uber and also to 'the smiling CEO' Ron Gutman. A trade news bulletin posted by Connie Loizos on 2 May 2018 announced the ouster of Gutman:

> Ron Gutman, the co-founder and CEO of HealthTap, a venture-backed medical advice startup, was reportedly elbowed out today by his board of directors. The reason, the board said in a letter to employees, was that it had finally heard too many complaints about Gutman's behaviour inside the company.
>
> ...... excerpts of an explainer provided to Gutman...alleges he "committed acts of intimidation, abuse, and mistrust and that [he] repeatedly mistreated, threatened, harassed and verbally abused employees."
>
> "This leaves us with no choice but to fire you," reads the letter. "The toxicity you introduced into the workplace ends now."
>
> (Loizos, 2018)

Gutman provided a spirited riposte to this letter shared openly by the Board – but it was all too late.

So in this case, the Board ejected a toxic CEO. Good to know it can happen.

But what happens if the Board itself is toxic? We will look at this question in due course.

5

SO WHAT EXPERIENCES HAVE REAL PEOPLE HAD OF TOXIC HUMANS AT WORK?

In this chapter, we hear stories from people who have interacted with toxic individuals at work, on Boards and in different sectors and industries. After each recollection, there are some key reflection points to invite the reader to discern patterns of behaviour and to selectively extract ideas for how to help others as well as themselves to cope in toxic work and Board environments.

UNIVERSITY IT DEPARTMENT

What Experiences of Toxic Humans Have You Had?

'There was a particular professor who made my life a misery. He was a bully – a full professor who looked down on me. Every interaction was just miserable. While the whole place wasn't toxic, obnoxious behaviour by professors was tolerated by the system. I was still under 35, and I could be feisty when it came to fighting back but as I recall those times, I realise now that I wasn't particularly skilled to deal with people like him at that time. The place was really a bastion of white male power where some believed they had the right to be "the elite". I was a young woman, and often the only one present at set-piece meetings. If I knew then what I know now in terms of how to handle conversations with such toxic humans more wisely, things might have been better. One coping strategy that I developed came via what I call the "wise secretary" with whom I would confer prior to going to executive board meetings. I learned how not to add oxygen to the fire – so if he chose to take me on about something, I would dutifully listen to him and then, when he'd finished, ask: "Is there anything else?" I would then wait patiently, and listen to more if more was said (all to ensure the oxygen was depleted). Then I would ask: "This is what I heard – is this right?" This approach helped to prevent the worst kind of shouting matches from developing. I also made sure never to bump into him on my own – more because I never wanted to be in a situation where what I might have said to him in a one-to-one situation might later be misrepresented – and with no one else there, no witnesses, I knew it would have been very difficult to dispute his version of events.

These days, I am interested in Board functioning and have gone through certification with Advisory Boards and hold membership with a professional Board institute, one that requires ongoing professional development. When I think of the executive Boards we had when I was a young university administrator cum lecturer, I can only imagine that the archetypes [discussed earlier in Chapter 3] would have featured strongly there! It seems to me that certain types of organisations are subject to different intensities around politics. I do believe that the more senior the person is, the more likely they are going to impact the organisation, and the more insecure these people are, the riskier things become – because the stakes are high. And so in this kind of environment, people have to evolve a way to survive. I never thought of quitting though I can understand why some people would, given the circumstances'.

Key Points

- Obnoxious behaviour is frequently tolerated by the system.

- Toxicity can exist in pockets – not necessarily the whole organisation.

- People discover the need to develop interpersonal communication strategies to deal with a bullying leader.

- As an alternative to quitting, people have to proactively devise a way to survive.

INTERNATIONAL EDUCATIONAL INSTITUTE

Do You Think Toxic Humans Shape Toxic Organisations, or Do You Think Toxic Organisations Shape Toxic Humans?

'In the case of the institute where I worked, it would be the latter i.e. toxic organisations shape toxic humans. In our institute, apart from the faculty, no one else mattered. I can't see that situation changing anytime soon. Some departments had very good leaders who managed to "save" their teams from the more toxic parts of the organisation. In certain circumstances, you might find that the whole team's very toxic and yet it manages to survive, somehow. Probably because the boss is toxic. It's not a nice experience to work in teams like this. If everyone allows toxicity within the team it will basically continue and deepen until someone decides to call it out. For things to really change I believe it has to come from the top. Without coming from the top, nothing else will have much effect'.

Key Points

- Toxic behaviour tolerated by the system.

- Some good managers try to 'save' or 'protect' their team from the worst excesses of a toxic system.

- For change to happen, it needs to come from the top.

- 'Us' and 'Them' dynamics in organisations are highly toxic.

GLOBAL CONSULTING COMPANY

What Is Your Experience of a Toxic Boss?

'I remember when the new CEO came in. He had a great vision but when I realised that he was in cahoots with the CFO in terms of manipulating the numbers, and when he asked us to say yes to his strategy, I really, really wanted to say No. At that moment of asking, I felt drunk without being drunk. It felt so bad. It left an indelible impression on me: you must be true and authentic to yourself but at the time I needed money, was under financial pressure and I needed to keep my job. On reflection, I see now that the CEO was a narcissist, aided and abetted by an easily manipulated sidekick – in this case the CFO. He was a very persuasive narcissist, our CEO, and also very adept at getting others to do his dirty work. He could be extremely charming but also frighteningly aggressive. He could fire you on the spot. I always used to ask his secretary in the morning about what kind of a mood he was in before attempting to talk to him. I always remember him saying to me with a smile: "I don't care how you do it, but I want a million dollars out of you".

All I could do was to keep my head down. If you were to say no, or disagree with anything, you would be out. I think that a lot of young and ambitious people find themselves in this situation – this was my experience. The boss was American and as far as we could tell, the management in the United States didn't care about us at all, and there was never any intervention from that side of the house. On the other hand, our local team bonded around our shared anxiety about this boss and even to this day, we remain firm friends! We coped together and looked after each other: we had each other's backs.

Much later in my career, I had an opportunity to catch up with my old boss, and he came close to admitting that maybe sometimes he'd got things wrong. But by that time of course, it was way too late'.

Key Points

- Even if your behaviour – by any measure – is toxic, as long as you are 'delivering', particularly against massive stretch targets, toxic behaviour is frequently tolerated by the system.

- Narcissistic bosses (charming and aggressive at the same time) use others for their own nefarious purposes, deliberately distancing themselves and often using a stooge or side-kick.

- Toxic humans often put us (ethically) between a rock and a hard place: they know our vulnerabilities (such as needing to keep the job to support the family), and they lose no time in exploiting those vulnerabilities.

- Sometimes, there is a silver lining where individuals with a shared challenge such as a highly intimidating boss – bond, and then band together for safety and protection.

GLOBAL FINANCIAL SERVICES COMPANY

What's Your Experience of Working With a Boss Who Displays Psychopathic Behaviour?

Sometimes, people say that they work for a boss who's a psychopath. What I think they mean is that they work for a boss who displays some psychopathic traits maybe – or is a particularly hard and harsh taskmaster.

In my case, I actually *did* work for a psychopath boss. Why do I say that? Well for one thing, I was warned from the outset. An older female colleague of mine – when I joined the organisation – said to me: 'You do know that Annie [not her real name] is going to be your new boss? Because of that, I need to tell you something. Do not cross her. She destroys anyone who crosses her'.

I'm the kind of person who always likes to give people a chance. At the same time, I like to challenge in a respectful way. The leadership team that I joined happened to be in a state of flux, people were coming and going: in all honesty I felt that some people had been there too long and did not, in my view, have the strategic capability to make the necessary changes aligned to our business strategy, so I embraced the changes. My new boss Annie came in as the leader of the team and immediately set about marginalising certain people and creating cabals. She seemed to make it her business to gather the more easily manipulated people (and lower capability/performing people) around her to form, if you like, a mini-power base. Within our team, one of my colleagues (let's call her Mary, not her real name) was at the time seen as the highest performing and highest potential leader, and on the succession plan for Annie's role, and it was clear from early on that Annie felt threatened by this new person, not because of any particular behaviour from my colleague but simply because of Mary's exceptional business feedback and capabilities. There were also increasing numbers of complaints about Annie coming from different people. It was gradually drawing on a number of colleagues that Annie wasn't actually any good at her job. The common opinion on Annie among multiple stakeholders was that Annie lacked depth of business and HR knowledge and capability with a focus instead on buzzwords and fluffy initiatives and very little substance. The complaints continued to pile up – so much so that Annie was put on a Personal Improvement Plan (PIP). Shortly after this, I moved to another part of the HR team and Annie brought in another person (Emma, not her real name) to backfill my position. Emma displayed highly toxic and racist behavior through several actions including claiming to multiple colleagues that 'there are too many Race X in this company'. Emma also took to deliberately marginalizing the Race X colleagues through several actions including *not* inviting one of the Race X colleagues to attend team meetings.

From Bad to Worse

Gradually things got worse. Despite the company wanting to fire Emma, Annie managed to muddy the waters by claiming Emma was being bullied. Annie also managed to concoct bullying allegations against Mary and eventually managed to get her 'restructured out', in other words, fired.

You might ask yourself how any global company manages to make these kinds of mistakes in the decisions they make. What Annie had done, as a psychopath would do, was smartly identify the few stakeholders in the LT (Leadership Team) who did not work much with Mary, and create a fantasy bullying story (with tears) which was enough to create enough 'evidence' to take the actions they did.

I think all of us have the capacity to lie. In fact I think all of us have a certain capacity to be toxic too. But the scary thing about Annie was that she was able to make up *whole new narratives from out of thin air*. You couldn't characterise these narratives as being a bit 'economical with the truth' or 'just' deliberately missing out or unintentionally overlooking bits of critical information. No. This was a lying narrative more akin to fantasy. Normal people don't make up the whole narrative out of nothing, passing off stuff that never happened as fact. I found this very shocking.

Making a Stand

I was so appalled at this behaviour; I decided to make a stand. I went to the Regional CEO and told him all about my concerns about Annie. As happens in such cases, the issue was referred to Global [HQ] and maybe, not surprisingly, Annie was moved on. But so was I. I think I was brave to do what I did, but in retrospect, I could have been more strategic and smarter. You need to be when you are dealing with people like Annie.

Annie at one point threatened to go public about how she was being 'victimised'. She said she had friends in high places in the media, and that it would be 'very bad' for the brand if she was to tell her story about how toxic our company was. So the company caved: they gave her a rousing farewell party and she gave a bravura, Oscar-winning performance about how much she loved the company. I was amazed at how easily the company colluded in this fiction. Annie was free to move on to another organisation – it was all as if nothing had happened.

Key Points

- Beware of leaders who use a divide-and-rule strategy *within their own* team to weaken it and make it more pliable.

- Be wary of individuals (especially those in senior positions) whose reputations go before them. There is a reason for that – and that in itself provides the rationale to be cautious in your interactions with that person. Some say 'A leopard never changes its spots' – again with good reason.

- Be brave and strategic – if you are going to whistle blow, try to ensure you have thought things through. Are you aware of the possible ramifications as the accused party bites back? Talk things over with a close confidante.

You are going to need to be brave and courageous but thoughtful in the action you take.

In this story, we heard about someone with deep-seated issues coupled with little self-awareness. The person's narcissistic tendencies, power plays and carefully engineered strategies to enable intimidation and undermining behaviour – made her a truly frightening person to be around. Her influence created toxicity, and it was fortunate that enough people managed to make enough complaints that the management had to act. Psychopaths in the workplace get found out eventually. The hope is that they get found out before they can achieve maximum mayhem.

GLOBAL HOSPITALITY IN ASIA PACIFIC

Experiencing Trauma at the Hands of a Bully

'There was this one leader, a senior leader who held a CEO-type type position in the APAC region. I happened to be doing a lot of work with his boss. There came a time when I needed to work on a leadership development initiative within his part of the business. This man's leadership style was incredibly dominant and overbearing, pushing people to beyond their limits really. At one point within the process he was shouting at different people, micromanaging them. For example, in the beginning, just at the outset of the programme, the chairs in the room had been arranged theatre-style. I said to this senior leader, "Do you mind if we rearrange the chairs into something better for dialogue?" He got very upset with me and said: "The theatre-style arrangement of the chairs in the room is how I like it". It took me 30 minutes to persuade him otherwise. His need for microscopic control extended to what position the chairs had to be in! Even before we started the 5-day programme! Added to this, we had to move locations to carry out the leadership programme for different groups in different geographies: frankly all of this was emotionally draining for me. There was nothing but incessant questioning and micromanaging.

In the end, we had to take him to one side. I decided to draw a line. I told him that I was not happy with the level of aggression exhibited by him – and given we were running a leadership development experience – we actually needed him to be a role model! My initiative helped to spark a conversation which eventually led to a kind of truce. I have absolutely no doubt that this man had already damaged a lot of people during the course of his career and certainly before I encountered him – bullying and intimidating his colleagues as he did, and adopting an extremely aggressive style. The strange thing is, though, he actually lasted quite long in the role. It seems that sometimes certain sectors condone or forgive such behaviour. He was quite successful in that industry: in fact, it was quite militaristic in nature – a full-on service industry. It's where the staff are expected to provide an amazing experience for their guests – *but the staff themselves are treated very badly*'.

Exploitation Is Rife in Toxic Environments

What this looks like in reality is that the frontline people are generally vastly underpaid and completely unappreciated by the owners of the businesses. These frontline staff often have a very close and constructive working relationship with their immediate supervisors who are in many cases stuck in the same situation. So in my view, it is not the immediate line managers who are the problem. The real issue is between senior leaders at the C-level and the frontline people, especially when it comes to pay distance. It is hypocritical to run seemingly meaningful town halls about how much you are a caring employer – when in fact your main objective is to pay your people as little as you can get away with, pay your C-level people very generously and enrich the very wealthy investors who are the actual owners of the businesses.

In other words, exploitation is rife in these toxic environments.

This is one of the reasons why there has been – and in my view, continues to be – a problem with recruiting into this sector – it's an issue that has been around for a long time, so my view is that this kind of 'cultural toxicity' has long-term, pervasive impacts which may not be foreseeable.

I still have memories of this person and flashbacks of working with him. The sad thing is that the piece of work itself should have been something that normally I would really have enjoyed, focusing on the participants and their experience, instead of babysitting the boss.

But I was quite traumatised by it and still think about it.

Key Points

- Toxic behaviour from our leaders often manifests itself in micromanaging and shouting behaviour.

- Toxic individuals will often justify their pernicious and vindictive behaviour by saying they are simply being professional, and that they make no apology for pushing their people hard (a typical justification from people who enjoy the power and the fact that they can make life very difficult for someone without very much effort on their part).

- Standing up to bullies. Bullies are themselves victims: standing up to them to 'spark' a conversation is a great thing to do – if you can do it. It is something that requires bravery and courage.

- Toxic organisational cultures have long tails, and their malign effects permeate the future. Allowing toxic behaviour to take root (now) may be bad enough – but we can be sure things will get a whole lot worse as our discerning talent pool of young people demands more ethical behaviour from senior leaders and indeed, board members too. These younger generations will vote with their feet.

GLOBAL ENGINEERING COMPANY

Have You Had Any Experience of Systemic Toxic Collusion?

'My experience at the hands of a toxic leader concerns a member of the C-Suite of a global engineering company. When he joined the company, and we can call him Colin, part of his induction involved having one-to-one meetings with all his direct reports and their team members. Colin was in charge of Group Strategy and Marketing for the company. So this was the good part – you could call it "Stage #1" of a particular process: trying to get a good sense of what people felt particularly about the strategic direction and marketing plans of the organisation. However "Stage #2" – and this is where the toxic part kicked in – was that during these one-to-ones, he would "profile" all of these people according to his own criteria, criteria unknown to anybody else. Through this process he would identify people as falling into one of two groups: the first group was the Informants or Spies group and the second group consisted of those people who he thought represented a potential threat to him. This could be because of the experience they brought with them or the competence they had, or their hunger and passion for change, for growth and innovation. Then came "Step #3". If you happened to be categorised into his Informants and Spies group, you were required to continuously give him valuable information about your team, what they were thinking and more especially what people (especially senior people) were saying about him, Colin. And if you didn't supply this kind of information, you would get a low performance rating at the end of the year – or he would try to get you kicked out. It was like, at the end of the year, you got the bill for being associated with him.

In terms of dealing with leaders such as me who fell into the second group, he made it a habit of praising our work when he was with us but sabotaging the work when he was not. To give you an example: this company had never really had a proper marketing think tank. Colin and I discussed how this could be put together and how it might operate. We decided to organise the first ever company-wide 1-day workshop with an invited expert speaker to help us think through how such a marketing think tank could be established. Then, just one day before the workshop was due to take place, Colin gave me a call and ordered me to cancel the workshop and terminate all of our planning. The only reason he gave was: "We have other priorities". So I had to call off the meeting and tell the expert speaker not to bother flying in to see us. And this episode literally marked the end of any kind of thoughtful marketing strategy for that organisation. So what had happened? Well, the company was divided broadly into three main business units with one of the units being the significant driver of revenue. This unit had its own SVP of marketing, someone who we can call Brian. What had happened was that Brian had called Colin once he had got wind of this idea to set up a pan-enterprise strategic marketing think tank and, sensing that his own power might be compromised by such a development, Brian had told Colin that he thought these plans for a think tank were pure b*******. He told Colin that he had to stop this thing in its tracks. Since both Colin and Brian had a "we inform and spy for each other's benefit" relationship, which was established when they studied together at university, Colin aligned with Brian and stopped me. (This might be a good point at which to underscore the fact that Brian and Colin had both attended the same university and had known each other for many years)'.

A Phone Call Out of the Blue

If we fast-forward a few months to my performance review, Colin told me that I had done a good job – although he had had an idea just now that it would be a good thing for me to join Brian's team – Brian had suggested to Colin to move me to a role over with him. They had a longstanding bond. But what made the experience so toxic was the following: out of the blue, I received a phone call from Brian's personal assistant who insisted that we needed to meet. I said, 'Sure, when would you like to meet?' And she said: 'Right now'. So I headed straight to a company café to catch up with her. Over coffee, she told me she had something to show me. She pushed a sheet of paper with the print face downwards over to me. 'Read it', she said. The print out consisted of a series of email messages chronicling an exchange between Colin and Brian about how to get rid of me. It was replete with bad language describing me. 'This guy is pretty good: he has ideas. But we need to get rid of him: he can be dangerous for both of us!' was the overarching message. In the exchanges, Colin asked Brian whether he had a plan. Brian said, 'We need to do something about curbing "his influence"', i.e. my influence. Colin went on to ask Brian if he had any ideas about how to exit me. Brian then made a suggestion: 'Offer him a role in my team to do a job which we both know he will never be able to succeed at – and then after a few months, I'll be able to fire him for substandard performance'. So this became their plan. I was puzzled as to why Brian's personal assistant would wish to share this with me: when I asked why, she said that she had seen this kind of thing happening too many times before and that she was sick of this culture. She said 'I can't stand being part of this anymore. It's been going on for years. They systematically destroy people'. We finished our coffees and left. She offered to leave the copy of the email exchange with me but I declined. I had seen enough.

True to the plan, I duly had my performance review with Colin at which he gave the impression that he 'just had a great idea' – namely that I could take my skills and benefit the company even more by moving over to Brian's team. I listened to what he had to say and then said: 'I'm afraid I will never work for Brian'. Colin was in shock: the company culture was to obey orders and follow recommended career steps. He retorted: 'Well then in that case, I can't guarantee you anything as far as your future in this company is concerned'. It was clear that both Colin and Brian wanted me out – or at least out of their orbit of influence. So I ended up finding another role in the company in a completely different part of the business. There was no overlap with either Colin's or Brian's political interests. Five or six years down the line, I heard that many of the ideas that I had proposed around strategic marketing for the company were now being discussed. Both Colin and Brian had gone. An old friend said to me: 'You were six years ahead of your time basically, your thinking was a threat to Brian who really didn't understand the advent of the digital age and he felt threatened by you'.

In terms of how I coped with all of this, I have to say I got very close to suffering extremely severe depression. I put on weight and became very conscious of what information I shared and with whom I shared that information. You could say that a kind of paranoia set in. I closed up, I felt vulnerable and I felt unprotected. One of my biggest reflections now is that the behaviour displayed by Colin and Brian happened by consent: in other words, they couldn't have done and said the things they did without the tacit consent of the system. Everyone knew this kind of thing was happening. It's amazing to me that both men felt perfectly safe to use company e-mail to discuss me. They didn't feel threatened at all. They used company systems to execute their politically motivated exit strategy for me.

It was a toxic mindset which basically operated like a criminal mindset.

Key Points

- Applying a set of criteria to a group of people to decide who is a 'goodie' (those I can manipulate) and who is a 'baddie' (someone who could threaten me or my position) – is a classic approach for toxic leaders.

- Some toxic leader behaviour is reminiscent of the reckless actions of psychopaths – such as the blatant use of company email to discuss how to engineer the sacking of someone.

- Collusion in the organisational system exists such that people, fearful of their own position, 'turn a blind eye' to what is going on.

- Good people will do what they can to stand up to unethical behaviour from leaders and others even at potential personal cost.

- Machiavellian plotting by toxic individuals can severely affect the mental health of otherwise strong and robust people through creating a sense of fear, uncertainty and paranoia.

- Survivors of toxic politics depend on a support system of family and friends who always have their back, no matter what.

- Victims of toxic work environments tend to pick their close supporters more carefully in future: they develop a deep sense of intolerance for negative people.

GLOBAL FINANCIAL INSTITUTION

Combatting Poisonous Leadership Takes Courage and a 'Never Give Up' Attitude

'I had moved from what was a healthy place to a work – admittedly a very challenging one – from a role in development finance. I had an opportunity to return to Germany after an extended period of time abroad – and was able to land a good job with a global financial institution in southern Germany. Despite being German by birth and growing up in more or less the same region as the one in which my new employer was located, my many years abroad had changed me, and so it didn't take me very long to work out that the culture in my new place wasn't really me. It also dawned on me that my experience wasn't really relevant to what the company had in mind as far as its future plans were concerned. It was as though I was hired because it seemed to everybody that I would fit in – but it turned out to be quite a fateful move.

On a particular day during a typically cold and icy winter, I arrived at the office at approximately 9:10 a.m. having gingerly navigated the slippery pavements of the city and stopping briefly en route to grab a cup of coffee to perk me up (after the previous night when I had worked until close to midnight). In the world that I had just come from, we had floating work hours – so arriving into the office – with no scheduled appointments – just shortly after 9:00 a.m. wasn't a big deal. I honestly didn't think it was. However, as I look back, I can now see that this was the start of something.

Why? Well, just after I greeted him, my boss looked straight at me, staring into my eyes and said frostily: "We start at 9:00 a.m. What happened?" My initial thought was that he was simply joking. But then I realised he was deadly serious. So I came to realise – rapidly in fact – that the culture of the organisation was very different to what I was used to.

Not long after that, I needed to share the news that I was pregnant. I decided not to take the long, legally permitted maternity leave and instead opted to stay away from work for just 6 weeks. I had figured that I had just started my new role and wanted to do right by everyone by taking care of the new addition to my family and contributing to activities at work. At the same time, I wanted to make sure that I would be able to breastfeed my new baby at my workplace – and so our au pair would bring the baby to me at the office. I paid out of my own funds to make all this happen. Then of course came the question: "Hello, any idea where can I breastfeed?" I know I can come across as quite pushy – I'm not shy. The company eventually ended up giving us the use of the first aid room. I would eat my sandwich there and then go and pump in the restroom'.

Toxic Environments Are Empathy-Free Zones

There was a total lack of empathy for my situation from anyone. My male colleagues let me know that their wives were all at home with *their* babies. I felt that people were inferring or insinuating that somehow I was making their own wives look inadequate. But I'm a great advocate for choice. And this is when things really started to go sour. First the CEO told me that I would need to improve my English, and while I thought that was an odd thing to say (given that I was educated in an English-speaking environment over many years), I thought oh, OK, if you say so. I did stand up for the projects I believed in even as they came under attack – so I didn't just give in to everything. But then my boss said to me that he would like to see me breastfeeding: that he would like to see my breasts. On another occasion, I managed to land a terrific business deal: the boss' reaction? He accused me of sleeping with the good-looking male lead on the client side to win the work. And all the while our team meetings continued where it seemed that the boss' goal was simply to spend the time shouting at us.

How You Yourself Can Degenerate in a Toxic Culture

'One day, I felt a flu was arriving, and I decided to stay home to cure myself. As I learned later, informing the employer by email of this fact was not enough: it needed to be communicated on paper and handed in, in person, to human resources, with a copy handed to the line manager. My company insisted on this and provided a legal warning. This is when I decided after months of harassment to seek legal advice. People said: "You realise if you do that, you will never work in this industry again, don't you?" But I pressed on. I drew inspiration, support and warmth from my strong female networks. As part of the dispute/resolution activities, my boss and I went through a mediation process during which time he simply kept grinning at me, winking occasionally. I also found myself hating myself for being toxic to my own team members: shouting at them myself from time to time, saying cruel and harsh things. I realise how pernicious a toxic culture with toxic leadership truly is: the longer you stay, the more you yourself degenerate. Toxic organisations make toxic humans.

In our company, we managed to develop a fully formed culture of fear where people were terrified of losing their jobs and where bad behaviour was normalised. A toxic environment is something we absolutely have to address.

I did win my case for sexual harassment in the end. I also found a better, higher position in the same industry. Yet, I wish I could have sparked more change. And do you know what? The boss is still there, still the shining star. There have been women before me and now, also after me, fighting the same battle around him, yet few dare to speak out and even fewer choose to defend their rights in court. Sometimes, I receive an occasional phone call from another woman in that company who needs a new job – there is so much suffering, and little change'.

Key Points

- Organisations that are ignorant or dismissive of diversity, equity and inclusion should be a red flag. This is a manifestation of deeper issues and does nothing to build cohesiveness and acceptance. It provides an opportunity for toxic behaviour to take hold.

- Toxic behaviour can be catching! Normalising bad behaviour is an example of the 'systemic toxic collusion' that pervades many organisations. People stand by while their colleagues are pilloried and penalised: they are simultaneously inhabiting a compassion- and empathy-free zone and enabling it.

- Strong human networks of friends and supporters are essential if you plan on taking on your toxic employer from a legal standpoint. Legal cases can take years to resolve, and without the love and support of the people nearest and dearest to you, it is very hard to cope and get through.

- This story pre-dates the #MeToo movement: it has aspects of gaslighting in it as well as cruel and insensitive treatment of ordinary people. It is a recollection of how difference can be weaponised to get rid of someone the organisation deems to be 'not a good fit'. So keeping records, sharing your experiences with people you trust and seeking legal advice – these are all effective ways to protect and support yourself.

GLOBAL MEDIA ORGANISATION

'Everyone Knew What He Was Like' – Systemic Toxic Collusion at Work

'An individual I know destroyed his senior management team (SMT). One of the team members must have lost 15 kg through stress while another ended up needing significant psychiatric intervention to help him. This toxic individual – the SMT leader - behaved in a way that could be considered sociopathic and I remember coming home one day and saying to my partner, "I have to leave".

This person took great joy in destroying people. He would consistently phone or message the team late into the evening, calling conference calls on public holidays ostensibly to discuss work, but really, these calls were a complete waste of time. It was beyond insane. He would threaten to destroy livelihoods and reputations. It was absolutely awful. As head of HR, I turned into a counsellor. People would come into my office and cry. What this individual managed to do was destroy people's self-worth and self-esteem.

People got to such a low point that they stopped even bothering to apply for other jobs because they were in pieces and didn't have the confidence to apply'.

Toxic Individuals Cast a Long Shadow

'I'm still in touch with some colleagues from that period, and to be honest, we rarely talk about that specific time. . . . . .but I only have to mention that toxic individual's name and people still flinch. He was able to survive because everything was devolved, and it was just a question of him reporting his numbers. There was no real oversight, and so people working under him felt that they had nowhere to go. Even when I raised him as being an issue, I was disregarded.

One thing I have noticed is that there are structures and protections which are put in place for junior people but not senior people, because we assume that the seniors can fend for themselves. When you're at the midpoint in your career, it may be more possible to find a new job – but if you're in the C-suite, it could take a year or more to find another position. Because of this, some people are more likely to tolerate toxicity precisely because they have fewer options available to them.

That period in my career was terrifying. I can even feel my heart pumping, telling you about it. He was like a malevolent gremlin. I am recalling right now the sheer joy that this person took in hurting people. He was just evil. I guess he was the most extreme case that I have come across. And what he was like was common knowledge in the organisation. Everyone knew what he was like'.

Key Points

- The toxic SMT boss in this story was known to be a terrifying individual. We often ask of these kinds of individuals in organisations: how do they get away with it? Here, part of the systemic toxic collusion we can discern comes from the actual structure of the organisation which made it easier for the man to stay hidden in plain view: his targets were his own team members, and yet he managed to bully and intimidate with impunity.

- There are reasons why people might put up with such bullying behaviour: if you are into the latter part of your career in an organisation, you might choose to suffer in silence because you believe you have no other options available to you.

- This individual took pleasure in tormenting his colleagues. And so while the incidence of truly evil people in leadership and management positions in organisations might be comparatively rare, this story shows that they do exist – and that their malign influence persists long after people have left the organisation.

- Such toxic individuals leave scars on others that may never heal.

6

SO WHAT APPROACHES DO WE NEED TO ADOPT TO MITIGATE THE EFFECT OF TOXIC HUMANS?

In this chapter, we will start to explore what kind of approaches we might need to take in order to mitigate the effect of toxic humans: in other words, what would we need to do to reduce the potential for a given organisational culture to enable the rise of toxic individuals, to manage toxicity when it occurs and then to deal with the effects of toxic behaviour?

THE ORGANISATIONAL PERSPECTIVE

Donald Sull and Charles Sull, co-founders of CultureX, have written extensively on toxicity in organisations, providing us with many fascinating insights from the research that they have conducted. Here's what CultureX focuses on in its work:

> Launched in 2020 and based in Cambridge, Massachusetts, CultureX delivers actionable insights organizations need to measurably improve their cultures. Harnessing cutting-edge artificial intelligence developed at MIT, CultureX measures culture with high accuracy and pinpoints concrete ways to improve. Based on decades of research and work with dozens of Fortune 500 companies, CultureX provides evidence-based interventions tailored to the client's unique needs.
>
> (https://www.culturex.com/about-us)

So can organisations really address toxic cultures? Here is a view from the Sulls:

> *Organizations can address toxic culture, but* **systemic and sustained improvements require top executives and corporate boards to commit to change.**
>
> (Sull & Sull, 2023)

The bold highlighted text underscores for me the importance of getting the Board and the senior management team (SMT) working in lockstep to do what they can to safeguard the health of the organisational culture. I will share in some detail in Chapter 8 some thoughts on organisational strategic initiatives that organisations, led by the SMT and supported by the Board, could take. For now, however, it is important to narrow down where our focus should be if we are thinking of tackling workplace toxicity. Donald Sull and Charles Sull observed through their research that a toxic culture can be broken down into five principal constituent parts. These are:

1. Lack of inclusion;

2. Disrespect;

3. Cutthroat behaviour;

4. Abusive management;

5. Unethical behaviour.

They also asserted in their report *The Toxic Culture Gap Shows Companies Are Failing Women* that women are 41% more likely to experience toxic workplace culture than men.

Source: Donald Sull and Charles Sull, The Toxic Gap Shows Companies Are Failing Women, MIT Sloan Management Review, 2023

The Sulls observed:

- Women spoke more negatively than men about most elements of culture, including work–life balance and collaboration.

- Employees in toxic environments are more likely to disengage from their work, exert less effort and bad-mouth their employer to others.

- Toxic cultures exact a dreadful toll on their victims. . .[such that] sustained exposure to a toxic culture increases the odds that employees will suffer from anxiety, depression, burn-out and serious physical health issues.

- Toxicity affects employees on a deeper emotional level than most other elements of the employee experience.

Donald Sull and Charles Sull, Gap Shows Companies Are Failing Women, MIT Sloan Management Review, 2023

In a different report called *How to Fix a Toxic Culture*, Donald and Charles Sull suggested that there are three critical drivers that organisations should concentrate their efforts on: unsurprisingly one was 'leadership', the second was 'social norms' and the third was 'work design'.

REFLECTIONS ON LEADERSHIP, SOCIAL NORMS AND WORK DESIGN

Leadership

One of the most disturbing instances of a failure of leadership and of chronic systemic issues in an organisation has involved the Metropolitan Police force (the 'Met') in the United Kingdom. This is the police force charged with safeguarding citizens in London and the London metropolitan area. In 2023, a damning report on institutional failures within this police force was published by Baroness Casey (a member of the House of Lords and a former British government official specialising in social welfare) and the committee brought in to look at the problems at the Met. In the report, which ran to more than 300 pages, the investigators shared the following harrowing details:

. . .discrimination *"is often ignored" and complaints "are likely to be turned against" ethnic minority officers, to the point where black officers are 81% more likely to be in the misconduct system than white colleagues.*

It concludes: "Deep in its culture it is uncomfortable talking about racism, misogyny, homophobia and other forms of discrimination".

The report also reveals:

- Dilapidated fridges were repeatedly found over packed, and when a freezer broke down during last summer's heatwave (in 2022), the evidence inside had to be destroyed, meaning cases of alleged rape were dropped.

- Discrimination towards female colleagues, bags of urine being thrown at cars, male officers flicking each other's genitals and sex toys being placed in coffee mugs.

- Initiation rituals included people being urinated on in the shower.

- One Sikh officer had his beard trimmed, another had his turban put in a shoe box and a Muslim officer found bacon in his boots.

- Almost one in five of Met employees surveyed had personally experienced homophobia.

> Thomas Mackintosh & Lucy Manning, special correspondent, written report, BBC News, 22 March 2023

This case shows just how toxic an organisation can become when its culture becomes 'rotten to the core' as the mother of murdered black teenager Stephen Lawrence describes it (BBC News report, 22 March 2023). It is a shocking reminder of what can go wrong when an organisation becomes truly toxic.

Social Norms

In their report *How to Fix a Toxic Culture*, the Sulls outline the following key areas for attention in terms of establishing healthy social norms:

- Let work groups define their own social norms;

- Have distributed leaders lead discussions of social norms;

- Collect credible, granular data on subcultures and leaders;

- Mine the powerful insights buried in free-text responses in employee surveys;

- Check in on a regular basis;

- Benchmark against peers and competitors;

- Measure microcultures at a granular level;

- Measure subcultures created by individual leaders;

- Make it safe for employees to provide useful feedback;

- Take action based on employee feedback.

> Donald Sull and Charles Sull, How to Fix a Toxic Culture, MIT Sloan
> Management Review 2022

We will refer back to these valuable insights and ideas in Chapter 9 when we identify and prioritise what actions to take to minimise, manage or contain toxicity in our organisations.

Work Design

We will also address the topic of work design in Chapter 9 when we look at Antidote Actions that senior leaders can take in order to mitigate the effect of toxicity in their organisations.

SHAPING AND SAFEGUARDING THE CULTURE OF THE ORGANISATION

During the course of this book, I have emphasised the important and pivotal role of the Board of Directors in helping to shape and safeguard the culture of the organisation. Likewise, Donald and Charles Sull believe that it is critical for the top team to:

- *Quantify the benefits of 'a cultural detox' to keep this item [organisational toxicity] on the agenda* – I also see this as an ongoing, work in progress item.

- *Publicly report progress to keep the pressure on* (this could be reporting of race, ethnicity and gender data connected with the organisation's DE&I initiatives) – I also think affirmative story-telling and story-sharing can be very powerful.

- *Model the behaviour you expect from employees* – in my experience, senior leaders more often than not underestimate the degree to which they are being observed by other junior colleagues in the organisation, which means that as a senior leader or Board member, you need to be keenly aware of the fact that people are observing and learning from you.

- *Track progress with honest data* – as often happens (in measuring empathy in an organisation, for example) there is a disconnect between what senior managers (and the CEO) think is being achieved and what is actually being achieved, i.e. senior leaders might think they are dealing quickly and decisively with the unethical behaviour of a given member of staff, whereas middle managers, in particular, can be less impressed. They are usually much closer to the issue and they have high expectations that things will be dealt with quickly (which is not always the case).

Donald Sull and Charles Sull, How to Fix a Toxic Culture, MIT Sloan
Management Review, 2022

About the pivotal role of the Board in dealing with toxicity – a mini-case study:

Plopsa – the Board takes action as Belgium reels from widespread organisational toxicity revelations in the country.

Plopsa is the theme park division of Studio 100 which in turn is a hugely famous Belgian business entity with four television companies and four animation studios, in addition to its theme park businesses. Its eight water-themed amusement parks are located across Belgium, The Netherlands, Germany and Poland. Plopsa's business is creating fun, but nothing could be less amusing than the unceremonious sacking by the Board of its CEO of 23 years, Steve Van den Kerkhof as a result of reports detailing the 'bullying culture' at Plopsa.

However, as a former employee points out, the toxic culture which developed at Plopsa under Van den Kerkhof seems by no means an isolated case in Belgian companies:

Ex-employee who testified about the CEO's behaviour:

Since my testimony a month ago, I have been inundated with messages from people who have experienced the same thing in one way or another, but not necessarily within Plopsa. Plopsa is a big name and so it gets into the press, but in many companies with a lesser name the same thing happens and that doesn't come to light.
(Régis D'haenens, VRT News, 21 March 2023)

So the problem of toxicity seems to be something of a widespread phenomenon in Belgian organisations. But back to Plopsa for a moment. What people in Belgium are asking themselves now is: Why after 23 years did the Board *finally* take action against the CEO? It seems that the toxicity in Plopsa had reached such poisonous levels that the Board could no longer tolerate or ignore the situation. It begs the questions: *So how many people would have suffered during two decades of such toxic leadership? Why was no one able to stop it? Or was it just a recent phenomenon?*

THE TEAM PERSPECTIVE

When we think about the team perspective on toxicity, one of the writers and thinkers upon whose work we can draw for some important insights is Patrick Lencioni, who is most famous for writing the bestselling management book *The Five Dysfunctions of a Team*.

Lencioni used the story of a fictional company to showcase some classic dysfunctions that we observe in a team context. These are:

1. An absence of trust;

2. Fear of conflict;

3. Lack of commitment;

4. Avoidance of accountability;

5. Inattention to results.

Lencioni's work was written against the backdrop of an imagined American company. For readers who have lived and worked in parts of the world other than the United States, the dysfunctions identified by Lencioni are still relevant and valid although they can show up in different ways, depending on the dominant country culture of the team in question. The one foundational golden thread which I feel runs through all teams, including multicultural teams, is the question of trust – whether it's there, in the process of developing, or in a state of disrepair. As we are aware, trust is something that can take time to develop – but it can be destroyed in nanoseconds. Trust is like a plant that needs light, earth, water and air around it for it to grow and thrive. If any of these items are missing or if the environment is toxic, then it will be very difficult for the plant to survive and thrive. Trust is what exists in teams of people who are co-creating it in real time: if any one of them is toxic, it will have an immediate and potentially unrecoverable, unbridgeable effect (https://blog.12min.com/the-five-dysfunctions-of-a-team-pdf/).

As an example of dysfunctionality in teams in action, we can use a Board example (given that a Board is a 'team' in a certain sense – although some might dispute this). Writing in Directors & Boards Vol 37 No. 5 Third Quarter 2013 (*The 'toxic' director: It takes only one to derail the Board*), George Isaac shares the following:

> *Having served on 25 boards, of which 14 were corporate boards, I have observed numerous examples of one director significantly derailing the effectiveness of a board. In certain instances... one director caused so much disruption that key Board fiduciary duties and directives got sidelined over less relevant pet-peeve issues or biases raised by a dysfunctional director.*
>
> (Isaac, 2013)

George goes on to say:

> *Toxic directors can come from any element on the board: the CEO, founders/owners, and inside or external board members. It only takes one toxic director to impact a board's effectiveness. None of the reasons for poor performance [observed by George] were due to incompetence of the board members but rather from* the softer issues of how directors function in a group. *Careful evaluation of these issues must be included in any assessment of prospective new board members.*
>
> (Isaac, 2013)

'The softer issues of how directors function in a group'. This is a helpful remark from George as it underscores the criticality of the power dynamics at play in this particular 'team' – one that we call 'a Board'. If the dynamics are toxic, that spells trouble. Likewise, George's point that 'Careful evaluation of these issues must be included *in any assessment of prospective new board members*' is a key insight.

BOARD INTERVENTIONS WHEN THE C-SUITE IS TOXIC

We have just considered the issues when the Board is toxic – as a result of the impact of just one toxic board member. What then of the role of the Board in terms of oversight of toxic SMTs (the C-suite)? Earlier we looked at the example of the CEO of the Belgian water amusement park company Plopsa. Annette Templeton writing in *Psychology Today* ('Boards Must Intervene to End Toxic Behavior in the C-Suite') shares the following story relating to toxic C-suite behaviour:

> *"With a promising strategy for growth and highly differentiated competitive advantage, the board of directors of a spin-off from a highly successful parent company hired a CEO to lead this exciting venture. She was a first-time CEO with impressive domain expertise and an inspiring vision. The legacy team members were also excited about what was possible – a meaningful mission and purpose and the potential of significant financial gain. Yet, within the first three months, the CEO exhibited toxic behaviours. She ignored and even belittled long time veterans. She lost her temper in large group meetings and dictated decisions that would significantly affect the company's clients. Many of the company's most valuable experts were threatening to leave.*
>
> *Concerned by the destructive behaviour of this newly onboarded CEO, the board decided to intervene – and the CEO was removed. This response to toxic C-Suite behaviour should be a model of best practice for boards, but, in truth, it is all too rare".*
>
> (Templeton, 2022)

My interviews suggest that the rarity of intervention by the Board in C-suite people dynamics is spot on. Many Boards are reluctant to get into what they see as 'management' of the C-suite and I think that is understandable: the watch-word for Boards is indeed 'oversight'. However, when you factor in the potential damage that an uncontrolled and potentially uncontrollable CEO and his dysfunctional team can do and how their toxic behaviour cascades through an organisation (this is 'poisonous leadership' in action), the reality is astounding. According to Gallup, the cost of toxic leadership to the US economy is up to $550 billion per year in lost productivity while SHRM (The Society for Human Resource Managers) puts it at $230 billion. Whichever way you look at it, these figures are enormous (Annette Templeton, Boards Must Intervene to End Toxic Behavior in the C-Suite, Psychology Today, posted 15 November 2022). At the very least, Boards need to demand data on employee engagement and they need to act when they discern issues in the making. They also need to observe the SMT in action and think carefully about what they see and hear. A throwaway remark, a put-down, a tendency to talk over someone – these are all signs that Boards should notice and not ignore.

C-Suite Interventions When the Board Is Toxic – Recollections From the Middle East (Beauty Sector)

Here, we share a story from one of the people interviewed for *Toxic Humans*.

'I moved to the Middle East and as part of my CFO (Chief Financial Officer) role, I was appointed as Secretary to the Board. This enabled me to have a full view of all the personalities on that Board. Fortunately the General Manager (GM) and I got on very well: we were joined at the hip, we had shared values. We were able to insulate our teams from the full pressure of the Board. I remember our very first board meeting was a complete bloodbath. It made me think, *how on earth do you run a Board and manage all the Board dynamics?* One thing I realised through my subsequent experiences is that you never stop learning. In our case we had a joint venture (JV) where the local partner was the minority in the JV. The board members came with big egos and of course, distinctive and individual styles. In the early period, I remember the pain of being publicly chastised and humiliated by some of these people. They seemed to think, "[As a representative of the majority partner], *you must listen to ME!*" It was Management by Fear, so they seemed to think that as representatives of the majority partner, they got to tell you what you should do i.e. you have to do as you are told.

From our perspective, the GM and I needed the majority partner members to understand that, given that the minority joint venture partner was extremely well-respected and had a significant presence in the region, you couldn't simply treat them like s***. So the toxic behaviour in the Board really started with the majority partner. I remember going for a drink with my GM after the first meeting, and both of us had the same thought: *what on earth happened in that meeting?* We were trying to answer the Why? What? & How? We needed to come up with some sort of response, some sort of way to create a *modus operandi* for the future. So together we devised a plan whereby I went to meet the minority partners in a social setting (over breakfast or lunch) and tried to establish what their pain points were. It was clear from the outset that the key factor was a lack of trust - as well as a raft of other issues. I then went to the majority partner members and tried to explain to them the perspective of the minority party members. The response from one of the board members to me was an acidic, "Hey you, just remember who's paying your salary!" I felt I had to respond in kind so I answered, "Well, I know this company has a hotline for reporting bullying and intimidation. So please remember that, too." I made the point (and I needed to reiterate this) that the task (and challenge) at hand was to galvanise everyone to move in the same direction rather than to expend energy issuing threats to each other.

I'm pleased to say that over time relationships improved. The GM and I were able to explain the grievances of the minority partner gradually and diplomatically to the majority partner. At times I have to say I felt like I was caught between a rock and a hard place. It also made me reflect on the actual process we would need to work to when meeting as a Board: first of all, we needed to ensure that there was always an actual formal agenda. In that initial bloodbath meeting there was no formal agenda. So I implemented this. I also started to produce pre-reads 7 days in advance of the board meeting. I enlisted the support of the Chairman to underscore to all board members that they had to read these pre-reads because part of our valuable Board time would be used to review the contents of the pre-reads. I would also meet each of the board members separately in one-to-one get-togethers and collect their questions ahead of time so that we could be better prepared. We also ensured that the practice of minuting the discussions was strictly observed – and I have to say, that part of the process had a significant and positive impact. So at the outset of the board meeting the Chairman would say, "Hands up all who have not read the pre-reads!" Of course no one would put up their hand. And so although it took time, it was possible – gradually and incrementally - to build trust. We made a point of channelling everyone's attention, energy and passion into focusing on what the competition was doing and emphasising that if we didn't move "as one", the competition would have us for breakfast.

The GM and I helped each other to manage our stress levels during the interactions with the Board. It's all well and good to have a drink together but you must control that. I made it a rule not to work on the weekends and to exercise when and where I could, just to preserve my mental wellbeing. Since that time, I have continued to work on my health and so my mantra these days is *Mind, Body, Soul*. By the time I left the Middle East and moved on to my next role, we had managed to reduce the board meeting time from 7 hours to three. I regard that as quite an achievement. It's also an encouragement to others to trust in the process and bring structure to the interactions with the Board - through this, you can develop trust and mutual respect. With patience and over time, this can become a kind of "virtuous circle" which enables respectful challenge balanced by authentic support'.

From this story, we can discern the following:

- Establishing a process and protocol for the Board to follow is essential – while this might be a well-understood aspect of Board functioning in some geographies, it isn't necessarily something that is widely practiced across the globe (hence the need for Boards to seek out guidance on good governance and effective Board practices).

- Go slow to go fast – if the composition of the Board is fragmented in some way, you need to take time to understand who's in the room, with whom they are aligned, what if any cliques or informal sub-networks exist and also, the individual histories of the people who make up the Board.

- Have courage and commitment – Boards are often collections of high-achieving, take-no-prisoners types of people which means you will need a thick skin and, drawing on the experiences of the duo we heard about here (the Secretary to the Board/CFO and the General Manager), having a close ally or buddy with whom you can plan and strategise as well as comfort and commiserate with – is going to be especially helpful.

- Remember to take care of *you* – preparing for and navigating a board meeting is no walk in the park. Take time to prepare but also to recuperate afterwards. Many board meetings that I have attended – or observed – have been truly brutal affairs: allow yourself time to process, relax and decompress.

THE INDIVIDUAL PERSPECTIVE

In this section, let's take a look at the individual perspective, reflecting on some potential sources of toxicity such as Fragile Masculinity and asking ourselves whether vetting or the use of psychometrics can help us in identifying potentially toxic leaders. We will also consider the role of coaching and mentoring as a possible means by which to combat poisonous leadership.

Fragile Masculinity as a Source of Toxicity

Maryam Kouchaki and her colleagues writing in the *Harvard Business Review* ('Research: What Fragile Masculinity Looks Like at Work', HBR, 26 January 2023) noted the following:

> *No one likes to feel like their identity is being threatened. Whether someone makes a flawed assumption about your religion, sexual orientation, or even just your favourite sports team, being treated like you're something you're not - can really sting...*
>
> *In particular, studies have shown that when men feel that their gender identity is being questioned or threatened, they are much more likely than women to respond by reasserting that identity through aggressive thoughts and harmful, toxic behaviours. A wealth of research has shown that masculinity is among the most fragile of identities, so precarious that even seemingly minor threats*

can push otherwise-ethical men to lie, cheat, harass, and even commit assault, all in an attempt to prove that they're "real men". But how do men react when their masculinity is threatened in the workplace specifically and what can organisations do both to reduce how often men feel these masculinity threats at work and reduce the harm caused to everyone when these threats do occur?

(Kouchaki et al., 2023)

Studies such as these are crucial if we are to exercise honesty and truth about where toxicity arises. Helping and supporting men to think about different ways to 'be a man' is something we need to address from when men are young and to offer a more variegated, nuanced and sensitive picture of what being a man is all about. This means challenging notions that compassion and empathy are somehow 'feminine' qualities – this is so unhelpful because we need men to buy into the idea that compassion and empathy is all about being a fair and just person – not a 'kind and gentle' person – and the strong message we need to put out is that displaying compassion and empathy must apply equally to all genders.

And while I have brought up the topic of Fragile Masculinity as a source of toxicity, it is also important to recognise – as we saw in Chapter 5 – that organisations are home not just to toxic male leaders, but female leaders too.

VETTING AND PSYCHOMETRICS

Being able to vet a person for potential toxicity prior to bringing them into your organisation might sound like a highly desirable thing to do! In reality it is always going to be challenging, given how differently toxicity can manifest itself – not to mention the ability of some individuals to cover up their behaviour and true nature. One person I interviewed said: 'Toxic leaders are amazing actors!' Another person referred to their toxic boss as being capable of Oscar-winning performances, including tears and heart-rending emotion (none of it, needless to say, was authentic). So what can be done to try to get at toxicity before it gets at you?

This is where we might bring in psychometrics to give us some of the insights we need to make the right decisions. So where a psychometric might suggest that a person is lacking in self-awareness and their communication skills are not well developed, such a person could benefit from coaching and leadership development: all things point to them being skilled in a technical sense but not so skilled in a human or emotional intelligence (EQ) sense. Psychometrics can provide a useful starting point for action.

THE POWER OF PSYCHOMETRICS

Psychometric tests are typically used in three main areas: intelligence, aptitudes and skills and personality. They can be used as part of what are commonly referred to as 'assessment centres' where you might be asked to carry out a set of tasks or activities to assess your suitability or 'fit' for a particular job. These usually augment the traditional interview (typically face-to-face conversations). This is where psychometrics are used for *assessment and selection*.

In the world of leadership development, psychometrics are also used for *individual (and team) development* purposes where the intention is to provide a person (or team) with valuable insights into their behaviour. It is an ideal way to help develop self-awareness, something which most leadership development practitioners regard as a foundational piece for all leaders. According to Psychometric Success https://psychometric-success.com/aptitude-tests/test-types/psychometric-tests/, there are over 5,000 different psychometric tests available today (April 2023). Here is a list of the Top 10 according to Practice Aptitude Tests:

1. Numerical Reasoning Tests;

2. The Myers-Briggs Type Indicator (MBTI);

3. Verbal Reasoning;

4. Mechanical Reasoning;

5. Spatial Reasoning;

6. Abstract Reasoning;

7. Cognitive Ability;

8. Situational Judgement;

9. Logical Reasoning;

10. Analytical Reasoning.

https://www.practiceaptitudetests.com/resources/10-most-common-psychometric-tests/

It's interesting to see the MBTI being called out: this was first developed in the 1940s and measures psychological preferences in how people perceive the world and make decisions.

Another 'classic' psychometric is the Fundamental Interpersonal Relations Orientation-Behavior (FIRO-B) instrument. As a tool, FIRO-B is extremely useful in helping people to understand their own behaviour and that of others. It is based on a theory (Fundamental Interpersonal Relations Orientation) developed by William Schutz in 1958. FIRO-B measures interpersonal needs on three scales: Inclusion, Control and Affection plus two behaviours: Expressed and Wanted. It helps people to understand, for example, how much you initiate a certain behaviour with others and what you tend to do in given situations ('Expressed') alongside how much you want others to initiate the behaviour with you, how much you prefer to be the recipient ('Wanted'). A report would shine a light on how you show up for people (very useful for self-awareness) and acts as a trigger for conversations on working more effectively with others. It is a useful resource for coaching too. If, for example, your need for Expressed Control is very high (on the scale 0–9, you score a 9) and your need for Wanted Inclusion is very low (say, 0 or 1 on the same 9-point scale), then you might start to see why some of your relationships might be fractious and how some people see you as a rather reserved, private person. Then you have choices as to whether you are OK with this or whether you think it is an area you might like to work on or develop. You might see the results as underscoring the need for you to work on your empathy, for example. This is why FIRO-B is an instrument for development.

Of course narcissists and those with psychopathic traits might well be very interested in their FIRO-B scores but whether they would be bothered about changing – is anybody's guess. I would suggest not.

So Can We Use Psychometrics to Discern Toxic People?

I think psychometrics can provide us with data on people to provide insights that enable good conversations to happen. However, as we know, there are different variables which combine to create the conditions for a human being to become toxic – or to exhibit toxic behaviours – and this means that we will need to take a holistic view of the different factors before formulating a response or an opinion. As I have mentioned in *Toxic Humans*, measuring a person's empathy may be one useful pathway – and there are psychometrics (measuring EQ, for example) which have empathy incorporated into them, as well as empathy tests themselves.

For those readers who wish to explore further, tools worth mentioning include:

Hogan – https://www.hoganassessments.com/about/
Hogan's approach 'provides the depth and detail needed to hire the right employees, identify and develop talented individuals, and build better leaders' through a suite of different psychometric products based on the Five Factor model (OCEAN: Openness to Experience, Conscientiousness, Extroversion, Agreeableness and Neuroticism). These 'Five Factors' are widely used by psychologists as a way to understand personality. Hogan's tagline is: 'We Predict Workplace Performance'.

Paradigm Personality Labs – https://paradigmpersonality.com/
Paradigm's 'WorkPlace Big Five Profile' also has its foundations in the Five Factors. It offers 'Profound Insights to Drive Optimization'. The 'Big Five' are referred to as 'Super Traits' – namely the Need for Stability, Extraversion, Accommodation, Originality and Consolidation.

Such psychometrics can generate valuable and useful data which, explained, interpreted and discussed by a professional skilled in that tool, can be immensely helpful. At the same time, their usefulness is contingent on people being open to considering aspects of their behaviour which they might need to work on. In other words, such tools may well provide the 'nudge' that some people need to effect a change – whereas other individuals, unfortunately, may choose to ignore what they read and conclude that they are getting their needs met by doing exactly what they are doing. The result is that they do not see any reason to alter their behaviour at all.

Lastly, one of the features to look for in psychometrics is what are known as 'derailers'. These are potential derailment factors that a person might wish to consider – behaviours that could knock them off-course. These derailment factors can often be surfaced through *360 degree assessments* (offered by a number of suppliers around the world) or by organisations like Hogan who look at the 'dark side' as well as the 'bright side', as part of the journey to helping people to become more self-aware.

In this chapter, we have started to think about the different approaches available to us to deal with or co-exist with colleagues who display toxic behaviours.

We will develop this over the next few chapters and summarise the key actions in our Toolkits in Chapter 9.

7

NOW WHAT CAN BE DONE FROM EARLY CHILDHOOD TO ADDRESS HUMAN TOXICITY?

In Chapter 4 we listed the elements of a possible conceptual 'Toxicity Equation'©:

Toxic Humans at Work = Genetic Predisposition + Environmental Shaping*
− Empathy + Systemic Collusion + Work Context

*childhood upbringing

We have touched upon the topic of Genetic Predisposition (see Chapter 4, p. 67) − let us now turn our attention to environmental shaping.

ENVIRONMENTAL SHAPING − UPBRINGING FROM CHILDHOOD

I think most of us would agree that what happens to us in our childhood has a significant impact on what shapes us as adults. So as we think about what shapes some adults into toxic humans, it seems to me that a reasonable place to start would be for us to think about early life experiences and to see what light experts on early childhood through to adolescence can shed on this fascinating area.

One psychologist whose work I follow keenly is the Canadian professor of psychology, Dr Paul Bloom. Dr Bloom has helped to popularise understanding about how children from a very young age are able to show care and concern for others, explaining that one baby crying will very likely set off another baby crying as a show of support and empathy. Very small children will show worry and anxiety about another little child who is crying: they will extend their hand and touch the other little child or they will offer to share their favourite toy with the little child who is sad and upset. It would appear that human beings have the capacity and ability to feel and show compassion from a very early age. Bloom has also written about the bias inherent in empathy – something we need to be mindful of – in groundbreaking books such as *Against Empathy*. So far so good.

But when we meet people as adults who are lacking in empathy and compassion – who perhaps appear between levels 0 and 5 on our empathy/toxicity continuum – what has happened to them? What life experiences have conspired to make them so toxic – or even so dangerous?

Our understanding and appreciation of empathy and compassion in small children is evolving all the time. While it was once thought that young children were capable of demonstrating unconditional compassion through to the start of their early teens, some recent research suggests that under certain conditions, the ability to do this starts to change around the age of four or five. In a recent study from Australia, scientist researchers in clinical psychology analysed the behaviour of 285 four- and five-year-olds and found that:

> ...children responded less compassionately to others when a personal reward was at stake.
>
> (Lu, 2023)

Scientists conducted an experiment involving asking young children to take part in a puzzle game for which they would receive a sticker as a reward. Puppets or adults played alongside the children, with the experiment set up in such a way that the puppets or adults were intentionally given too few pieces to be able to complete the puzzle within a given time. The puppets and adults expressed distress at their inability to complete the puzzle (as they had insufficient resources i.e. pieces) which gave the children plenty of opportunity to notice their anguish (that of the puppets and adults). As the study's lead author Dr James Kirby, a senior lecturer in clinical psychology at the University of Queensland, explains:

> *Across all of the studies we did, whenever they had extra resources, the children always helped... But when you give the child [just] enough pieces for them to complete it [the puzzle] themselves, that's when they don't help [others].*
>
> (Lu, 2023)

The scientists used different approaches to see what might improve the likelihood of the child giving up one of their pieces to someone else and found that they were more likely to do so if they had already received a sticker and would therefore not lose their reward!

The research team surmised that:

> *For young children, personal cost appears to be a greater inhibitor to compassionate responding than who compassion is directed toward.*
>
> (Lu, 2023)

For me, a key observation by Dr Kirby was:

> *At that age [four to five years of age], the brain is still going through a huge rate of maturational growth... [As scientists] we can inadvertently set up environments which turn off helping behaviour. [However in] environments where rewards can be won for certain tasks and there's only a limited number of rewards going around - what you're setting up is a competitive mindset.*
>
> (Lu, 2023)

This is interesting as it gives us a clue as to how such a phenomenon (scarcity of resource, leading to compromised compassionate giving, plus the emergence of a competitive mindset) might be one of the early triggers that start to contribute to shaping the individual in a particular way in later life.

FORMATIVE SHAPING AND 'SECURE BASE'

One of the giants of early child psychology is John Bowlby (1907–1990) who was the first of what are known as the Attachment Theorists. His proposal (to be known as Attachment Theory) was that the nature of the bonds children develop with a significant caregiver in very early childhood (or not) will have a profound impact on the rest of that person's life in terms of how they relate to other people. Bowlby's work and that of Mary Ainsworth in the 1970s and 1980s gradually led to the development of the concept of 'Secure Base', and eventually the extension of the concept to include adults (Michael Jenkins, Expert Humans, Emerald Publishing page 54–55). In my book on altruism, compassion and empathy (Expert Humans, 2021), I shared the following details about 'Secure Base':

> The work [Secure Base] has been further built on and developed by George Kohlreiser, Susan Goldsworthy and Duncan Coombs in their 2012 book Care to Dare: Unleashing Astonishing Potential Through Secure Base Leadership. In the book, they define "Secure Base" as:
>
> A person, place, goal or object that provides a sense of protection, safety and caring and offers a source of inspiration and energy for daring, exploration, risk-taking and seeking challenge. (2012, p. 8)
>
> One of the many reasons this is so important is that a secure base gives a person the inspiration and energy to be able to step out of their comfort zone and explore their unfulfilled potential, safe in the knowledge that their efforts to innovate and try new things, will be supported, and any failure they might happen to experience will not result in castigation or punishment.

Clearly, the establishment of the secure base in childhood is a critical factor in the shaping of the adolescent and the subsequent adult. At the same time it is unlikely to be the only determining factor in the eventual shaping of a *toxic human*. It seems to me that the lack of a secure base in combination with other factors (genetic for example) is the genesis for later difficulties and challenges. And it is worth recognising that not every human being who lacks a secure base will grow up into a toxic human! Research shows for example that orphans or successful people who lost a parent or both parents during childhood often go on to enjoy great success in adult life: indeed for some, it is this lack which is sometimes seen as the key driver or motivator to strive for the top.

I reframed this lack and linked the experiences associated with it using the term 'Hidden Gems', as explained in *Expert Humans*:

What do we mean by "hidden gems"?

I decided to use the term "hidden gems" to denote those life events or experiences that shape us as altruistic, compassionate and empathic beings – or not. Hidden gems could be positive experiences that yield positive outcomes – or negative, challenging experiences that can be turned into positive ones as we grow and develop as adults and members of groups, teams or organisations.

Amongst the negative and often traumatic experiences people can go through in early life is the loss of a parent. In her book The Fiery Chariot *from the 1970s, the writer Lucille Iremonger noted the high incidence among British prime ministers of having lost a parent in their formative adolescent years. 25 out of 40 prime ministers had suffered this loss, from Sir Robert Walpole in the 18th century to Neville Chamberlain (the prime minister at the start of the Second World War). In the US, we can discern a similar phenomenon: George Washington, Thomas Jefferson, Bill Clinton and Barack Obama all lost their fathers when they were youngsters. Abraham Lincoln lost his mother when he was only nine.*

(Jenkins, 2021)

This reframe of a lack (of a secure base) as connecting to 'Hidden Gems' in one's life experiences is intended to be an optimistic way of looking at things. As we try to understand what shapes toxic humans, however, the picture is not one of optimism.

It is more a story of bleakness, tragedy and often, horror.

LACK OF SECURE BASE: WHEN THINGS ARE EXTREME

In his book, *Making a Psychopath*, Dr Mark Freestone tells the story of Danny who suffers from a psychiatric condition called borderline personality disorder. It is a condition which is recognised in the American Psychiatric Association's Diagnostic and Statistical Manual of Mental Disorders (DSM). This condition involves a person who is agonised and traumatised by a lack of identity. Dr Freestone describes Danny's early childhood years, which eventually led to a series of foster homes (some of which were caring and others not so), involvement with gangs and eventually physical violence against others, landing him in prison and then psychiatric hospital:

> *Danny came into the system young. His father had been highly abusive towards his mother and older brother before leaving the family for good when Danny was a small boy. His mother, who seemed like someone trying to make the absolute best at being dealt a terrible hand in life, struggled with poor mental health, probably exacerbated by the physical abuse from her ex-husband and later partners...Danny's brother revealed that when Danny was a baby, their mother had stored him in a drawer in the desk in the house to hide him from his father's wrath (although when Danny confronted her over this later she flatly denied it). When Danny was eight his mother was judged unable to care for him and Danny was taken into foster care.*
>
> (Freestone, 2020, pp. 144–145)

This is an example of where abuse in early life shapes the individual and where systemic challenges – and sometimes sheer misfortune – combine to bring further harm to a person who may already be suffering from a mental disorder. I have deliberately chosen the early life of Danny as an example of what happens all too often in societies around the world: my purpose in doing so is to invite us to think about what has happened in the past to those toxic humans we encounter at work, in organisational life and on Boards. Perhaps what we experience (and suffer) at the hands of some toxic humans in the workplace has its origins in an extremely bleak, disruptive or abusive childhood. In this sense, combatting toxic humans becomes more an issue of first understanding them and then creating empathetic and compassionate responses to help them. I think it is something worthy of consideration.

So this is where we can start to think about the many varied and calibrated responses possible: on one end of the spectrum there will be extremely damaged individuals who need life-long support in secure institutions and who we are unlikely to meet in an ordinary work environment – and then there will be others in organisational life who are simply difficult to work with and unpleasant to be around (but who we may still be able to coach and support to become more collegiate members of the team). An individual like the officer in the UK Metropolitan Police (the 'Met') who spent the best part of two decades terrorising and raping women who trusted him – is an example of a supremely poisonous person who was able to use his position as a policeman as well as leveraging endemic and systemic shortcomings at the Met to achieve his terrible aims. We will examine 'systemic toxic collusion' later – this case was one in which people react with incredulity at what happened – 'How come nobody noticed?' I think that the idea that, as a cunning and charming psychopath, it would have been difficult to have stopped him earlier – is something that makes questioning the toxic environment hugely important and necessary if we are to try to protect people into the future.

OTHER 'SHAPING FACTORS' – SCHOOLS, BOARDING SCHOOLS, BUSINESS SCHOOLS AND TEACHERS

Schools and Boarding Schools

There are people who as children were sent away by their parents to boarding schools and who will say that it was a positive thing which taught them independence and resilience. Others will say that their boarding school experience was the worst thing that ever happened to them. There are what we call Third Culture Kids (TCK) – some of whom rejoice in the multicultural mindset they have as a result of their diverse heritage and experience ('a blessing') – whereas there are other children of globe-trotting expatriates who say their parents deprived them of an opportunity to grow up in a small provincial town or exciting city in their home country in which they could feel they had 'roots' ('a curse'). In 1989, David Pollock defined and described the TCK as:

> ...a person who has spent a significant part of his or her developmental years outside the parents' culture. The TCK frequently builds relationships to all of the cultures, while not having full ownership in any. Although elements from each culture may be assimilated into the TCK's life experience, the sense of belonging is [often] in relationship to others of a similar background.
>
> (Van Reken et al., 2017)

So if you are a TCK, your life experiences are going to add a further layer of complexity to the puzzle of what shapes people as individuals. And as an adult, if you are working in an international context, your TCK upbringing might provide you with valuable insights. Equally, moving around endlessly throughout your childhood and early adulthood might enable you to establish your people networks quite effectively in a brand new environment – but these relationships might end up being fairly shallow as your personal history means that you are exhausted at having expended valuable emotional energy on developing deep friendships in the earlier part of your life, and at this point in your career, you decide not to do that anymore. And this might cause others to experience you as superficial or unwilling to share what you are truly feeling and thinking i.e. as a human being you have developed a 'shell' and you stay resolutely inside it. People might find you cold, somewhat reserved, maybe even (unfairly) unfriendly (their 'perception' of you is their 'reality' of you). My point is that your life experiences to date will have shaped you, imperceptibly, into who you are at that period in your life. So for example, boarding schools can teach you resilience but in so doing, they can also make it very hard for you to admit your vulnerabilities and ask for help. And therefore, for some individuals, such early childhood experiences can cast a long shadow.

Business Schools

In my research for *Toxic Humans* I was fortunate to be able to talk to a number of committed and amazingly talented psychologists. Here's what one specialist shared with me in the context of the shaping of adults through the education system and specifically, the contribution of the traditional western business school:

> *I've had a hypothesis that the Business School system has contributed and is culpable [in developing certain kinds of leaders]. This part of the education system would be where leaders are supposed to have been trained. Where leaders learn how to reduce toxicity [not generate it]. But going to business school is a bit like going to prison: if you go to prison, people tend to get even more criminalised. Business schools are like that. Their focus has been on MBAs and increasing people's salary levels. In my opinion, the education system has not done well in this area. It focuses on developing a certain kind of intelligence – when what we should be after is what I would call "whole intelligence".*

If you come from a toxic family, school won't necessarily change anything - because you're in a Darwinist environment. You might be lucky to have a teacher who can help in a behavioural sense - coaching you on how to be a better human being – if you're lucky.

I think it is encouraging that the more progressive business schools are addressing the issue of how to develop more human leaders and to include support and instruction in this critical topic area. This was not the case in past decades. I recall a conversation many years ago with Henry Mintzberg who was a pioneer in questioning the value of a business school education in the format that such programmes were appearing in at the time (Henry has been a long-term critic of the traditional MBA programme). He was adamant that in MBA education terms, we were not focusing on the right things (this was discussed in his 2004 book *Managers not MBAs*). That was 20 years ago. And yet I still meet business school leaders who are among the last of a generation of educators who really don't get how important the development of leaders as humans really is.

Their time is now over, thankfully.

Which brings us neatly to teachers.

Teachers

I think most of us would agree that teachers play an extraordinarily important role in shaping children for the future. We have all got our favourite stories of teachers who we thought were wonderful and who gifted us a life-long love of, for example literature, or drama, or physics. And then we have our stories of the toxic teachers too: people who should never have been allowed to be in the company of children let alone teach them. My memories of school in the 1970s and 1980s are punctuated by violent events: teachers hitting schoolmates – even picking them up by their collars and throwing them against a cupboard or asking the children to vote on whether an underperforming child deserved to be beaten with a sports shoe (they always voted for the beating). Such memories stay with you, for ever, I think. And these will have shaped those unfortunate individuals into the future – of that I have no doubt.

BULLYING – AND HURTING ANIMALS

Bullying is one of the things that children remember – either as victims or observers. I think it is a 'big ticket' human behaviour that we experience as small children, throughout our teenage years and into the workplace as adults. We looked at some examples of bullying behaviour in the workplace earlier on in Chapter 5.

There are also children who, in their younger years, hurt animals – and who grow up into adults who enjoy making other people's lives a misery at work – or doing far worse. However, there are of course important distinctions to be made, as Joni E. Johnston of *The Human Equation* points out in her article for Psychology Today, *Children Who Are Cruel To Animals: When to Worry*:

> *Every act of violence committed against an animal is not a sign that a person is going to turn out to be a homicidal maniac. Particularly with young children, whose natural exuberance and curiosity can lead to some unpleasant experiences for their pets, it is fine to shrug off the occasional lapse in judgment while continuing to educate the child about humane animal treatment. However, locking a pet inside a closed space, violently lashing out at a pet after getting into trouble with a parent, or taking pleasure in watching an animal in pain are all "red flags" that signal the need for professional intervention. This is particularly true when the child has the cognitive maturity to understand that what s/he is doing is wrong, and repeatedly does it anyway.*
>
> (Johnston & The Human Equation, 2011)

One of the challenges we have in understanding the drivers for the toxic behaviour of toxic leaders in senior teams or Boards is that for the most part, we have relatively little visibility on their childhood histories. This means we have to look for other clues. This is what led me to look at other childhood experiences or considerations in an effort to gain some possible insights.

So for example, there are identifiable childhood trends that *might in later life* make people successful entrepreneurs – and we can maybe learn from them. These are detailed in Table 4 below.

Table 4. The 6 Childhood Trends of Successful Entrepreneurs.

Childhood Experience	About the Effect of the Experience	Comments
1 Experiencing change or disruption	Moving schools or an unnerving event – this disruption can help develop resilience. Mechanisms developed to deal with these disruptions become the framework for every future obstacle	Change can be a good thing for *some* people. As we have noted, moving country can prove to be a great experience for some whereas for others, it can be something they wish they could have avoided
2 Understanding the big wide world	For entrepreneurs, a sense of perspective is invaluable – 'zooming out' helps you to see what really matters	Many will have had experience of living overseas – so they get to see how others live. They bring a diversity of thought into organisations which can be incredibly valuable. This is a powerful impetus for imagination – imagining what might be possible
3 Awareness of work	Successful entrepreneurs had an early introduction to the world of work with dinnertime conversations helping to shape an understanding of how business works	Looking at the early life of the Chinese tech entrepreneur Jack Ma and founder of Alibaba, one learns that he would cycle more than 25 kms from his village into the city of Hangzhou in order to be a guide to foreign tourists and thereby to hone his command of English – and make some money!
4 Inquisitive with a desire to learn	Children who became entrepreneurs are characterised by their obsession with asking 'Why'? They especially enjoy taking things apart and putting them together again	While every parent knows about their child's propensity to ask 'Why?' it seems that the superpower of curiosity is at work here for the entrepreneurs-to-be. Importantly, curiosity and empathy are closely identified with each other ('curiosity before empathy')
5 Independence	The entrepreneurs studied were regularly 'thrown in at the deep end' – and once they had tasted independence they looked for it consistently thereafter	I noticed here that these entrepreneurs developed an ability to 'push themselves' and to keep going – not just an indication of resilience but of focus and determination

Table 4. (Continued)

Childhood Experience	About the Effect of the Experience	Comments
6 Role models	It was found that the friends and family members they met when they were small had a profound impact on their ambition and future reality	This underscores the immense value of role models in shaping childhood experience. In as much as the successful entrepreneurs had positive role models, we can see in the case of toxic human development, either the complete absence of role models (in particular, fathers) or role models that were themselves, toxic

Source: Table based on an article by Jodie Cook, The 6 Childhood Trends of Successful Entrepreneurs, Forbes 18 May 2018 and adapted with comments by Michael Jenkins.

Equally, there are some aspects from these childhood trends that could account for how people with these traits are experienced by others in later life – potentially in a negative way or perhaps *in extremis* – even in a toxic way.

LEADERS AND CHILDHOODS

Jodie Cook's valuable research and report on childhoods and entrepreneurs gives us an insight into what can shape successful innovators, inventors and business people. So while I was struck by the clear positives (see Table 4), it also seemed to me that some of these successful outcomes for entrepreneurs might also appear differently to people with a different childhood and background and be experienced differently by them. One of the outcomes of a peripatetic childhood (Item 1) is that the person might find it easy to strike up superficial relationships with other people but not wish to expend energy on developing relationships to a deeper level (having done this throughout their life to date, only to move on and have to start building connections all over again in the new place). People with this kind of childhood history may be perceived by some as unwilling to disclose much about themselves or to be painfully reserved: not evidence of toxicity you might say, but something that can create distance between people at work.

With Item 3 (Awareness of Work), we may have another possible indication of how a person with such a background might regard others who do not share the same kind of profoundly deep-seated obsession with work – to the point of regarding them as lazy. Elon Musk may be an example of such a person: his work ethic is legendary. An anecdote to illustrate this relates to how one day his personal assistant (PA) asked him for a salary raise. He suggested she go off on a short vacation. While she was away, Musk evaluated whether he could take on her workload and after a bit, decided he could. The PA returned from her short vacation and was fired upon her return. Toxic behaviour from the boss? You decide! (https://www.educator.com/news/why-elon-musk-fired-his-long-term-assistant-who-asked-for-a-raise/).

Another example: the relentless focus that we see in Item 5 ('Independence') may have some consequences when that focus collides with the behaviour of others who do not share that same focus or drive. It might not create toxicity necessarily, but it might cause interpersonal friction of a kind that *could* result in a person with this level of drive being experienced by others as obsessive and perfectionist in a way that can *start* to feel toxic to some.

Finally, I am reminded of a story about Richard Branson that would appear to underscore again the power of the item in our table above – Item 5 ('Independence'). It's a story of being 'thrown in at the deep end'.

Richard Branson

From an interview with *Business Insider* magazine, 18 November 2016.

> *When Richard Branson was around six years old, he was in the back seat of his mother's car on his way to visit his grandmother. With about four miles to go, the future billionaire founder and chairman of the Virgin Group started acting up – and his mother, Eve, stopped the car, pushed him out and told him to find his own way there [to his grandmother's place. Which he did]. As Branson recalls: "She was incredibly supportive, lots of love, but every opportunity she had, she would push us to the limits".*
>
> (Business Insider, 2016)

Is this character building – or child abuse? What do you think?

8

NOW WHAT CAN ORGANISATIONS DO TO ADDRESS AND MANAGE THE INFLUENCE OF TOXIC LEADERS AND TOXIC HUMANS?

In this chapter, we will start to look at what organisations can do to tackle the malign influence of toxic humans and toxic leadership. To do this, we will reflect on the negative consequences of *Systemic Toxic Collusion* and look at how toxicity can impact people during the various stages of their career in an organisation.

SYSTEMIC TOXIC COLLUSION (STC)

In their fascinating paper 'The toxic triangle: Destructive leadership, susceptible followers, and conducive environments', Art Padilla, Robert Hogan and Robert B Kaiser showed how three principle areas (or 'domains') come together, with their associated elements, to cause destruction (and toxicity):

1. Destructive Leaders;

2. Susceptible Followers;

3. Conducive Environments.

We have seen in Chapter 2 how narcissistic leaders behave, while in Chapter 5, our stories of toxicity in organisational systems and of toxic

leaders in Boards and senior roles – underscore the elements we see represented in Fig. 1 below – especially a lack of checks and balances and the
existence of ineffective institutions. It is also worth noting the mention of
'charisma', which has been the target of a lot of bad press in the management
and leadership literature. I think that charisma is a two-sided coin – positive
on the one side but not-so-good on the other. Tomas Chamorro-Premuzic
wrote an excellent article in the *Harvard Business Review* about *The Dark
Side of Charisma*. Here's a particularly fascinating extract:

> *Charisma disguises psychopaths: Although you don't have to be a
> psychopath to be charismatic, many psychopaths are charming, and
> the main reason for this is that their charm hides their antisocial
> tendencies, so that they manage to get away with it. Egocentricity,
> deceit, manipulativeness, and selfishness are key career advances in
> both politics and management, and many leaders rise to the top*

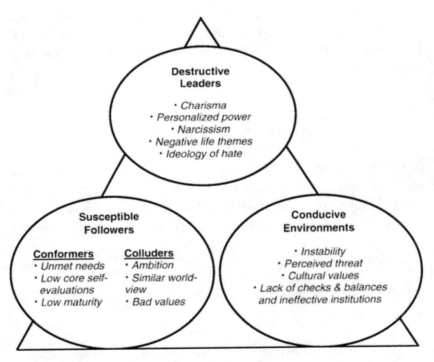

Source: Padilla et al. (2007, pp. 176–194).

Fig. 1.   The Toxic Triangle.

motivated by their own problems with authority. Although being in charge is a good antidote to having a boss, if you cannot be managed you can probably not manage others either – this is why Rupert Murdoch and Donald Trump spent very little time working for others, but too much time managing others.

(Chamorro-Premuzic, 2012)

Back to Padilla, Hogan and Kaiser's research: the work represented here is part of the field of 'destructive leadership' and it is interesting to see that the notion of different elements (leaders; followers; environments) coming together to create toxic humans, systems and experiences was being articulated as far back as 2007. On the surface it might seem that after getting on for two decades, not a lot has changed. The writers of the research paper suggested that 'Potentially destructive leaders might be identified in the hiring and promotion process by including assessments of narcissism and other dark side personality factors' (2007, p. 189) – something we touched upon in Chapter 7 and that we will look at again shortly. This is also something suggested by Chamorro-Premuzic as well:

Select leaders using scientifically validated assessment tools, instead of relying on "chemistry" or intuition. For example, narcissists tend to perform well on interviews and confidence displays are often mistaken by competence. Conversely, robust psychometric tests will identify character flaws in aspiring leaders and provide a reliable estimate of their likelihood of derailing – unlike humans, tests are immune to charm.

Padilla, Hogan and Kaiser also proposed that '….destructive leadership should be studied in its natural ecology, in terms of the interactions among leaders, followers and contexts' (2007, p. 190).

Let's do just that now – looking at context and seeing how toxic, destructive leadership can show up.

THE EMPLOYEE JOURNEY

Most people who work for an organisation will go through what is popularly known as 'The Employee Lifecycle' – a journey through different stages of organisational life. This is something that human resources people think about a great deal, as each stage of the employee lifecycle drives different activities and decisions – especially for HR people and the leaders they support. It is also something that board members ought to factor into their duty of care when it comes to thinking about what elements or ingredients come together to create what we recognise as 'the culture' of the organisation.

For these reasons, I thought it would be interesting to look closely at the employee journey and to consider how toxicity comes into the picture. Where i.e. at what stage and under what conditions might toxicity flourish? Do people enter organisations in a state of non-toxicity and as a result of different experiences take on different intensities or layers of toxicity? Do some people start work with organisations as 'fully-formed toxic humans' so to speak?! Are there ways in which 'the system' allows toxic humans to develop, become powerful, dangerous and damaging? Are there ways to detect toxic humans in such a way that we can avoid them joining our organisations in the first place? So many questions to consider! And in due course we will also be pondering a question which I believe is of great importance to us all – *how can we manage to live and work with toxic colleagues?*

DIFFERENT VERSIONS OF THE EMPLOYEE LIFECYCLE

There are various permutations in existence that broadly cover the different stages of the Employee Lifecycle. Most include the following five: Recruitment, Onboarding, Development, Retention and Exit. I like the two additions to the classic Employee Lifecycle made by Qualtrics, namely 'Brand Attraction' at the start of the cycle and 'Advocacy' at the end. Let's take a look at each of these seven stages through the lens of toxicity and how it affects people at work (Fig. 2).

Brand Attraction

I once attended an Interbrand seminar in which the speaker, Rita Clifton, controversially said that brand was more important than people – because 'brands last longer than people'! Coca Cola was cited as one example on

Fig. 2.   The 7 Stages of the Employee Lifecycle.

account of its longevity. It was a bit of a tongue in cheek comment but it
made the audience sit up and pay attention.

There is little doubt that toxicity and brands go together in the sense that
negative memories have a nasty habit of lingering in the public consciousness
long after the adverse publicity caused by various kinds of disasters or scandals
has passed. Some brands of course disappear entirely as a result of heading
straight into an existential crisis (we can recall Enron and Sunbeam from early
chapters in this book) – and then more recently, there are companies like The
Weinstein Company and Theranos that went out of existence as a direct result of
extraordinarily toxic behaviour on the part of their founders. Some companies
and organisations have managed to weather headwinds to continue operations
but many would argue that once the brand has been damaged in a profound
way, it will take a long time, if ever, before the brand recovers. Volkswagen as a
result of the diesel emissions reporting scandal is one example; Johnson &

Johnson and baby talc is another. For older people, Nestlé and contaminated formula milk remains a memory whereas younger people might not be aware of this scandal at all. But it takes a long time for bad publicity to fade. Hence, the delicate nature of brand. And organisations are keenly aware of how brands can attract or repel not only consumers but talent.

As Educational Data Systems, Inc (EDSI), a US-headquartered specialist in employer branding, puts it:

> *Employer branding ultimately helps attract top talent by offering candidates an up-close look at what your company is all about. A strong employer brand enables candidates to "self-assess" for fit within your company, which can increase employee retention and engagement rates over time.*
>
> *Having a strong, positive employer brand means that job seekers want to work for you. Why will a qualified individual choose you over your competitor? Good employer branding ...encompasses everything from free coffee to high-end bonus packages, from the physical space to the culture that exists within a company's walls.*
>
> (EDSI, 2023)

Today, many organisations deploy a variety of strategies to reach and appeal to the biggest generational employee demographic, Gen Y or The Millennials (75% of the workforce by 2025) as well as factoring in Gen Z expectations and increasingly thinking about Gen Alpha (entering the workforce in about 5–8 years from now). These include:

- Humanising your brand;

- Prioritising messaging around your organisational culture;

- Shining a light on specific employees to showcase talent;

- Creating a supportive environment to enable positive stories to emerge;

- Putting purpose centrestage.

Adapted from *Forbes* magazine article: How to build a strong employer brand that attracts top talent, 10 May 2022 https://www.forbes.com/sites/forbescommunicationscouncil/2022/05/10/how-to-build-a-strong-employer-brand-that-attracts-top-talent/?sh=32f58c472f99

Just by reviewing these employer branding strategies, we can start to see how organisations are effectively trying to neutralise any hint of toxicity (in an organisational culture sense) by focusing on the positives and strengthening their messaging around 'being human' i.e. signalling that their culture is anything but toxic. The key is to do this with authenticity and to be able to substantiate what you are saying your organisation stands for. For example, a company that champions sustainability as a way to reach and attract great people will want to avoid any reputational staining caused by accusations of 'greenwashing'. That is why – among many considerations for modern organisations today – sustainability reporting has become more critical and requires the utmost care to execute. So at this stage in the Employee Lifecycle, when the organisation is interacting with a broad audience – among which there could well be future employees – thinking about who gets put forward as a spokesperson for the organisation is an important thing to get right. From the get-go of their interaction with the organisation, people will be making judgements about it based on how the person in front of them comes across. The person who represents the organisation therefore needs to be carefully chosen – not always easy, especially when resources are lean or when it happens to be a small or medium-sized enterprise. As an interpreter, I have seen organisations put forward people who were unsuitable to be the face of the company – and that can hamper progress, particularly in joint venture discussions because it affects trust. I once interpreted for a Japanese company seeking to purchase land for building purposes in the United Kingdom: the British vendor representative was a loud, boisterous and aggressive individual who, from the moment he spoke to the Japanese side, put his own company at a disadvantage (because he sabotaged the potential for the development of trust from the outset). He declared: 'I heard you people [Japanese people] like to chit-chat before formal discussions because you want to be friends – I read it in a book about business etiquette in Japan – so let's chit-chat and let's be friends!' Unsurprisingly, the Japanese side was nonplussed by this bizarre greeting – but they kept their cool and proceeded with the discussions which were, frankly, tortuous. Our British vendor friend turned out to be as toxic as they come: warm and charming one minute, cold and ruthless the next. Quite a roller-coaster. I made a mental note to be chary about that particular property agency and to do my best to avoid it in the future!

Recruitment

I think that many organisations aspire to be a talent magnet and there are good examples of companies that achieve this through a combination of well-thought-out strategies to reach out to and connect with the talent that they are looking for. Key ingredients are a strongly articulated purpose; clear values; a commitment to learning and development; a commitment to take a stand on issues that matter to people such as sustainability; a well-articulated diversity, equity and inclusion (DEI) stance coupled with a commitment to creating a sense of belonging in the organisation; a strong social media presence to create an authentic and compelling story around care and a reputation for being a flexible workplace that is both human and humane. Salary and benefits are clearly part of the equation although research shows that *toxic work cultures* are more likely to cause a person to quit and move on – than salary:

> *A toxic workplace culture is by far the strongest predictor of industry-adjusted attrition and is 10 times more important than compensation in predicting turnover.*
>
> (Sull, 2022)

This underscores the importance of leaders at Board and senior management levels paying attention to the evolution of the organisational culture: if toxicity sets in and it is something that the organisation becomes known for, it also ratchets up as a significant business risk because the best talent will not want to join a company which is known for its poor work culture, even for a short time. What people are looking for in summary is a compelling employee value proposition (EVP) – a strong EVP. What is it that the organisation is offering in terms of personal growth, the kind of people you will get to work with, what kind of culture would you become part of, how meaningful will the work be and what kind of package is on offer – these are some of the questions that a good EVP will seek to address.

And Are We Sure About the People We Are Bringing Into the Organisation?

So what about the talent itself, the people we are bringing into our organisations? How sure are we, as we seek to ensure a non-toxic culture, that we are not in fact bringing the wolf into the fold? Is there a way to safeguard the organisation in some way against bringing in toxic humans?

I think the answer is: easier said than done. Some people may well be toxic before they join the organisation whereas some may develop into toxic individuals of varying toxicity, over time. Is there a way to tell if your applicant is a toxic person? Well, as we know, many organisations have for years attempted to screen their candidates with numerous and varied, and extremely sophisticated ways of assessing people for all kinds of qualities, traits and competencies. The depth and nature of these assessments can vary enormously as you would expect, depending on the kind of sector or job you are recruiting for. As mentioned earlier, 'Assessment centres' or processes designed to put people through a battery of tests and assessments – have been in use for many years now. These are often run alongside multiple interviews while requiring people to take on tasks of various kinds (such as preparing a sales pitch or giving a presentation about the company and its offer or products). What all these things do is give the recruiting organisation a good snapshot of the person they are considering via the selection process – striving to get the best picture possible with the tools and methods they are able (and can afford) to use.

The Traditional Interview

The traditional interview is a bit of a fixture for most organisations despite the recognition that interviews are vulnerable to all sorts of bias. In its excellent fact sheet on selection and associated processes and procedures, the Chartered Institute of Personnel Directors (CIPD) references a report by Anderson and Shackleton that calls out the following weaknesses of the traditional interview:

Weaknesses of the traditional interview

Self-fulfiling prophecy – *Interviewers may ask questions designed to confirm the initial impressions of candidates gained either before the interview or in its early stages.*

Stereotyping effect – *Interviewers sometimes assume that particular characteristics are typical of members of a particular group. In the case of sex, race, disability, marital status or ex-offenders, decisions made on this basis are often illegal. However, the effect occurs in the case of all kinds of social groups.*

Halo and horns effect – *Once interviewers rank candidates as 'good' or 'bad' in some aspects, they often replicate this judgement across the board, reaching unbalanced decisions.*

Contrast effect – *Interviews can allow the experience of interviewing one candidate to affect the way they interview others who are seen later in the selection process.*

Similar-to-me effect – *Interviewers sometimes give preference to candidates they perceive as having a similar background, career history, personality or attitudes to themselves.*

Personal liking effect – *Interviewers may make decisions on the basis of whether they personally like or dislike the candidate.*
(*CIPD Fact sheet*: Selection Methods, 2021)

This serves as a reminder of how unreliable interviews can be and holds true for Board selection too. I think Boards are particularly susceptible to the 'similar-to-me' effect (even though many will dispute this).

A friend in the human resource (HR) community also suggested to me that we should trust in the power of our own instincts – so if something feels 'off' in an interview – it normally is. Food for thought.

Screening for Psychopaths? Assessment in Selection Versus Assessment for Development

Short of conducting Bob Hart's Psychopath Test, I am not sure that current approaches to assessment and selection would necessarily identify a candidate as a psychopath! At the same time, by conducting different tests (psycho-metric tests), it is possible for the organisation to get a good idea about the psychological make-up of the individual – especially his or her emotional intelligence (EQ). It would also be possible through careful interviewing and observation to gain even deeper insights into someone's way of thinking and attitudes. All of this is done with the primary goal of assessing for fit – fit with the requirements of the job and fit with the culture of the team or organisation. It is all about potential. If we wanted to assess someone for *potential toxicity* I think we would have to approach the task tangentially – assessing them for empathy, for example, might be one route to consider. Many psychometrics today that are used for development (not assessment) are exceptionally insightful and helpful for individuals who want to develop themselves in various ways – and are best used when they can be interpreted and explained by an expert in the use of that tool or a coach or HR professional who has been trained and certified to work with it (as we discovered in Chapter 7). Such tools help people to see the different elements in their leadership skills repertoire and allow them to make informed decisions about what aspects they might like to work on and improve.

As a sober reminder of how important the question of fit is, the scandal-hit Confederation of British Industry (CBI) has learnt how critical the screening of potential joiners to the organisation is, as reported by *The Guardian* newspaper:

> *The Confederation of British Industry has admitted it failed to "filter out culturally toxic people" from its ranks, leading to "terrible consequences" including allegations of sexual harassment.*
>
> *The CBI president, Brian McBride, said in a letter to its members that the organisation has "made mistakes" and "badly let down" its staff, after a series of revelations in the Guardian about alleged misconduct by employees, including two women who were raped.*
>
> *The future of the organisation is now hanging in the balance, McBride said, saying he simply did not know if members would be able to "consider trusting us again".*
>
> (Isaac, 2023)

This crisis has become an existential one for an organisation that, for 60 years, has acted as the voice of British business. The CBI membership, on which the organisation relies as a main revenue stream, has deserted it in droves. As we have noted, it only takes a small number – even one – toxic human, to cause havoc and destruction. Therein lies the importance of bringing into the organisation, to the best of our ability and knowledge, the most appropriate people we can find.

As one of my interviewees, a senior Chief Human Resources Officer (CHRO), said:

If I'm selecting for a very senior person then I do full background searches beyond just the tick box exercise and I never rely on the recruitment agency. I will contact the previous employer and do a market check to see what kind of reputation that applicant has. I will also do what I can to find people who worked with that person. You've got to be prepared to go really deep. In fact I sometimes use a risk management company because frankly we can't take the risk of choosing someone who is not going to work out. If something goes wrong and it turns out they did something like that before – that's not an ideal situation to be in.

Onboarding

The experience of joining an organisation – the onboarding process – is something that many organisations take great care to get right. Onboarding as a topic is a rich area in and of itself: there are so many subtleties and layers around first impressions and meeting (or exceeding) the expectations of the candidate/newly hired person. There is definitely a way to do it and a way not to do it! It is important that the organisation and specifically the team that the person is joining are aligned to welcome the new arrival and to get the person comfortable with the systems and processes, tools and procedures necessary for them to do their job and to become productive in as timely a way as possible. Many organisations conduct post-onboarding surveys of new recruits so that they can identify any weaknesses in the process and thereby improve things for subsequent hires. Some organisations with programmes to support the employment of people who are cognitively diverse know that these colleagues will require more help and support – they will need to be located (in an office context for example) in a way that is suitable for them from a noise, heat and light perspective. Likewise new colleagues who have a physical need that demands special consideration will welcome – if not expect – an onboarding process that takes account of their situation.

When I was onboarded for my very first 'real' job in Japan, the HR guy charged with settling my wife and me into life in a big Japanese corporation – thought it was 'character-building' to listen in to me on the phone trying desperately in my rudimentary Japanese to arrange for the water, gas and electricity to be connected.

He could have done it in a few minutes but he said it was 'good for my Japanese to try'. Instead he stood outside the telephone kiosk, smoking, while I tried to make myself understood to various bored utilities call operatives: I was jet-lagged, it was the height of summer (hot and humid) and my Japanese was still fairly basic at that time – so for me it was a lousy experience, a toxic moment which stayed with me the whole of my time working for the company.

Development

The power of learning and development cannot be underestimated in terms of its ability to provide meaning and motivation for both newly arrived employees and people who have been with the organisation for some time. When asked why they decided to leave the company, people will often say that they did not have any real opportunity to grow and to learn new things – the job had become predictable and repetitive, lacking challenge and stretch. People in most cases relish the opportunity to upskill or reskill themselves – it makes them more marketable should the time come for them to leave their current employment while at the same time, making work more interesting. The people development industry is enormous as we know, with providers of all shapes and sizes providing development and training of every kind. I think it is useful to think of people development as sometimes involving *pure training* i.e. on how to operate a particular machine – and sometimes *pure development* – such as leadership development for someone who has been recently promoted as a first-time manager-leader. When we think of toxicity (ranging from mild to truly poisonous) – where someone is acknowledged as a person for example with great technical skill but who still has hard edges that need smoothing – initiatives such as one-to-one coaching or mentoring can be very helpful. The company might even decide that sending the person on an open (public) leadership development course could be of value. Then there will be other programmes that are fixtures in the L&D strategy of a company such as New Manager Pro-grammes (transitioning from being a sole contributor to a team leader for example) or courses that prepare people to go to the next level of the organi-sation (team leader to department director, for example). Such programmes will often feature psychometrics to help people understand themselves better and to gain a more detailed sense of what areas of their management or leadership style they need to focus on (to improve). The more targeted the development can be, the better – from the perspective of time, opportunity cost and financial investment. This is why most organisations that are serious about people development will make time to conduct a needs analysis ahead of any development for a particular group because different groups at different levels in an organisation will naturally require different things. Sometimes – when people are being evaluated for their suitability to attend a particular programme, attention will be paid to how they are doing in the organisation currently – what things do they do well; what things do they struggle with; how good and effective are their people skills – and so on. And it is at this point that the line managers of these programme candidates start to really think about how their team member is doing: are they fast and effective but do they leave a trail of destruction e.g. does their team exhibit above average levels of attrition? Could there be some toxic aspects to their leadership style which need attention? Do they tend to dominate and hog the limelight and put themselves forward as the star performer who made things happen, when it was really a total team effort? This is where I believe hints of toxicity can become apparent.

The biggest problem is when the origin of the toxicity lies not in the middle manager segment of the organisation – but further up the hierarchy among leaders who never go on leadership development programmes (they do not regard themselves as needing such things) and who would never think of hiring a coach or finding themselves a mentor, let alone engaging with a personality psychometric! We will address some possible solutions for supporting such potentially toxic leaders in the next part of this book.

Retention

The importance of purpose and values really kicks in at this stage as does the need for leaders to keep their finger firmly on the pulse of how their people are thinking and feeling. This also goes for the Chair of the Board in ensuring that they have a sense of how the CEO is doing – not solely from the viewpoint of results and achievement of objectives but also from the perspective of the CEO *as a human being*. CEOs also need developing and nurturing – and as we know, the top position is often characterised as a lonely place to be. Many CEOs also mistakenly think that they need to have the answer to everything – the more progressive ones realise that they can never know everything and that is why having a strong Chief Financial Officer (CFO), a strong Chief Human Resources Officer (CHRO) and indeed a strong Senior Management Team (SMT) is essential. People are increasingly open to the notion of CEOs sharing their vulnerabilities as well – but at the appropriate moment and not all the time! There are a number of global and local organisations that exist to support CEOs – not just for networking purposes but for mutual support and sharing (peer to peer coaching). It is relatively easy to find such organisations.

Exit

Progressive organisations are clear about the importance of a 'good exit', such that we are able to lay the foundations for the person who is leaving to possibly rejoin the organisation at a later stage in their career. That pre-supposes that the exit has been well-managed by the person's line manager and that the atmosphere that has been created around the point of exit is cordial and professional – and that HR has done a good job of supporting the exit process.

Unfortunately exits are often extremely messy. I was always struck by how brutal American exits are – people being escorted off the premises with their cardboard box containing photos of their family (that they have had on their desk in front of them, perhaps for years) and the bric-a-brac of a corporate life finished (paperweights from old clients, a pencil case with pens that have run out of ink, old publicity brochures, plastic boxes of your own unused business cards which probably should just be thrown out, lanyards from conferences attended for the past several years, etc.). My American friends have smiled as I relate such things and mention how I regard them as incredibly demeaning and insulting – and they say well, a lot of these rituals are laid out in a process manual which we absolutely have to follow to the 'T' less we trip over (and contravene any labour or employment laws). At the same time, I can imagine that if you had been marched out to the car park under the gaze of the 'survivors' up in the office block behind you – that there would be very little incentive at that moment in time to see yourself as a 'boomerang' that is going to come back some day. Never say never as they say! And having said that, I am reminded of the words of those I interviewed for *Toxic Humans* where people shared time and again: 'The place was so toxic there was nothing to be done. I just quit, as I have done once before when things got really bad' [Frances]. Another colleague shared: 'Sometimes if you work at a succession of toxic companies you kind of assume, well, that is what work is. That's what a workplace is. But now that I am in a small company that I love, with a boss who is fantastic, I can see the difference that good leadership makes. It has been like night and day for me'.

We can see that the exit is often the end point of a toxic experience for many people. People feel there is no alternative but to leave. Our task is to do what we can to try to turn this around and at least try to ensure that we are doing what we can to combat poisonous leadership as and when we see it – and experience it.

Advocacy

How well do people advocate for the organisation they have left?

This is going to depend on a number of factors. The first and obvious one is how good their experience was during their entire journey with the organisation: if they have had a good experience (or *mainly* good experience) at each stage of the employee lifecycle, all the way through to the exit stage, the likelihood is that they will be good if not great ambassadors for the organisation's brand. The recency effect felt by many human beings is such that someone's last day in their workplace is one they are likely to remember perhaps for the rest of their lives – so that is another reason for making sure that the leaving rituals are both respectful and humane. Great brand ambassadors can be worth their weight in gold in terms of recommending other good people to their old company. On the other hand, having disgruntled or angry employees – whose experience lands somewhere on the spectrum between poor to dire – may well mean that the organisation needs to brace itself for some serious blowback. This can take the form of furious messages on workplace reputation apps or social media: it could also take the form of ongoing interaction with former colleagues consisting of undermining emails that provide a channel for expressing ongoing grievances, frustration or anger. In extreme cases we know of instances where employees have exacted revenge on former workplaces in some of the worst ways possible. So the stakes can be very high if the process is not handled appropriately and the necessary countermeasures put in place. Threats of retaliation of a legal nature through cease-and-desist letters, for example, are unlikely to deter those ex-employees who continue to bear a grudge. They may have suffered from a toxic work environment but equally, the source of the toxicity could well have been them.

On a positive note, those leavers who are ready to leave or are moving on to something better or more challenging or that pays better – may be happy to be included in a work alumni forum where they are updated on what is new and happening at their old place of work and get-togethers are organised from time to time. This is a more uplifting type of ending than the vicious and grim scenario I have just shared.

COMBATTING TOXICITY AT DIFFERENT STAGES OF THE EMPLOYEE LIFE CYCLE: ORGANISATIONAL STRATEGIC INITIATIVES

Table 5 summarises some of the possible strategic initiatives that organisations could put in place at each stage of the employee lifecycle with the overarching objective of creating a more human workplace and combatting poisonous behaviour from top to bottom; the aims of those initiatives are also included together with some of the key actions that could be taken.

Table 5. Combatting Poisonous Behaviour at Different Stages in the Employee Life Cycle – Strategies.

Stage	Strategic Initiative	Aim	Action
1 Brand attraction	*Positive Outreach*	To create a non-toxic brand with appeal	Put people and their stories centre stage and showcase them – thus enabling outsiders to identify with insiders
2 Recruitment	Thorough screening and vetting of 'Best-Fit' talent*	To minimise bringing toxic people in	Adopt state-of-the-art assessment and evaluation; leverage AI advances – for Boards, be sure to use a Competency Matrix*

(Continued)

Table 5. (Continued)

	Stage	Strategic Initiative	Aim	Action
3	Onboarding	Prioritise 'Belonging' from the outset	To foster psychological safety and trust to combat toxicity	Ensure an optimal, human-centred joining process – and ensure that there is some kind of thoughtful induction process for new board members too*
4	Development	Learning and Development as 'Talent Glue'	To create a 'learning culture' to support and strengthen psychological safety as a toxicity antidote; for Boards, develop the sense of balance between support and challenge (recognising that too much harmony in Boards can be toxic too)!*	Create focused, innovative, intergenerationally sophisticated learning initiatives (to include Board and senior leadership development workshops) that simultaneously build skills (digital and other) plus human skills such as empathy and compassion*
5	Retention	*Alignment of Organisational Purpose and Values with Individual Purpose and Values*	To champion positive behaviour and call out toxic behaviour*	Create fun and meaningful staff (and Board) conferences (staff away days and 'advances') to strengthen Purpose; strengthen values through storytelling and sharing*
6	Exit	*An Eye to the Future*	To ensure a smooth and human departure for employees and proper 'end of tenure' rituals for board members	Pave the way for positive memories and potential return by employees; minimise scope for toxic misbehaviour post-employment
7	Advocacy*	*Keep Connected*	To develop a legacy ecosystem connecting past, present and future	Complete the cycle, with advocacy dovetailing with brand attraction to produce a Virtuous Circle

Items marked with an asterisk indicate that this item could be applied equally to Boards and senior leadership.

These seven organisational strategic initiatives (featuring in Table 5) can work as a starting point or inspiration for building your own strategy to combat toxicity.

What we are aiming for is a *preventative* approach:

1. Positive Outreach (for building a positive brand);

2. Best-Fit (finding non-toxic people to join you);

3. Belonging (building solid DE&I foundations to support the development of trust);

4. Talent Glue (building critical skills and the right conditions for psychological safety);

5. Alignment (aligning Organisational Purpose/Values with Individual Purpose/Values);

6. An Eye To The Future (ensure a human and humane departure to support future return);

7. Keep Connected (build an alumni ecosystem to connect past and present to the future).

In the next chapter, we will take things a stage further to ask: what can we do to manage or live with a toxic colleague?

9

NOW WHAT CAN INDIVIDUALS DO TO MANAGE OR LIVE WITH A TOXIC COLLEAGUE?

THE 'NATURE' OF TOXICITY

Phaik Ai Choo heads up Corporate Solutions for a Singapore-based organisation which brings leadership and talent solutions into for-profit and not-for-profit organisations. I asked Phaik Ai what toxicity meant to her and she shared the following:

We need to consider the "nature" of toxicity – it's a kind of feeling that you lack oxygen in your life; you can't breathe, it pulls you down, you feel empty. You start thinking: Is it me? Could I or should I be doing things differently?

So self-awareness is key. Having a tribe is key! Your tribe can help you to see things more clearly. And you need to be in touch with yourself. If I am unaware that what I really need is oxygen, then I wouldn't go looking for it. So connecting with others and learning how to use your emotions as data rather than letting them overtake you – is the name of the game. You learn how to be OK with your emotions.

It was good to get that idea of tribes, of networks of friends and supporters, underscored and validated as being critical in any struggle against poisonous leadership and toxic humans. Phaik Ai added:

Who is in your tribe is very important. Your family will always be on your side. And it can often be useful to speak with a neutral party, like a coach or therapist – someone who can be objective and help you to see a way through.

I asked Phaik Ai whether she thought toxic humans really existed. She shared with me that she believes that people are inherently good and that the emergence of what we might term 'toxicity' is a function of environment and upbringing – a view with which I agree. Intriguingly, Phaik Ai also said that from an organisational development (OD) perspective, it is the system you're in as well as the structure (i.e. organisational structure) that can also affect behaviour. This was an interesting idea and made me wonder how exactly organisational structures can influence behaviour: could organisational structures even be responsible for creating the conditions for toxicity to emerge in certain contexts?

I know from talking to stressed people in organisations that 'matrixed' organisations can sometimes create certain tensions which require careful management (a matrixed organisation is one in which individuals report to more than one manager – indeed they can sometimes have multiple man-agers). In my work as a facilitator, I am frequently told by organisations that they want to improve their often highly matrixed culture and 'make it work'. Success in a matrixed organisation seems to be contingent on getting aspects such as role clarity and shared expectations on objectives – right. It also seems to be affected by the *quality and nature* of the (often) multiple interconnecting human line management links. Allowing toxicity to enter this delicate equation is something we would want to avoid, given the already quite complex nature of the structure.

Another factor – when we consider the effect of structure on shaping organisational culture – is quite literally the structure in which the organi-sation is housed, i.e. the buildings which house the organisation. A classic example of this is the story of how, after the Second World War, which saw Britain's Commons debating chamber in the Houses of Parliament destroyed by incendiary bombs, there was an opportunity to redesign the chamber to make it less adversarial in nature (whereby the two major parties face each from two sides of a rectangular room). It was Winston Churchill who insisted on retaining the adversarial structure of the debating chamber, thereby perpetuating the confrontational flavour of debate and rendering a more collegial style of interaction more or less impossible:

> *Churchill insisted that the shape of the old Chamber was responsible for the two-party system which is the essence of British parliamentary democracy: 'we shape our buildings and afterwards our buildings shape us.'*
>
> – From UK Parliament: The Palace's structure
> https://www.parliament.uk/about/living-heritage/building/palace/
> architecture/palacestructure/churchill/

So in this sense, the structure of British parliamentary buildings has itself helped to perpetuate an atmosphere of aggression and toxic behaviour (if you would like a flavour of this, just tune in to Prime Minister's Questions [PMQs] on Wednesdays when Parliament is in session and you will see for yourself how even the design of a room can contribute to the shaping of a particular culture). It is no wonder that an organisation like Compassion in Politics https://www.compassioninpolitics.com/ was set up – something needed to be done to advocate for a better way of behaving in British politics – and a more respectful and civil way of interacting with others.

And so as we continue our reflection on organisations and toxicity, and individuals and toxicity, Phaik Ai introduces another interesting idea about 'Use of Self':

> *Toxicity starts from people. The leader is 100% responsible and "Use of Self" is a vital factor: leaders role model desired behaviours in the workplace and I believe they have the power and influence to show how an organisation should behave.*

'Use of Self' is an OD term to which I referred in my book *Expert Humans* and I believe this is one of the tools in the toolkit that we can use to help us in our interactions with people more broadly – and toxic humans more specifically:

> *Mee-Yan [Cheung-Judge], in a blog article in 2018 entitled What more does OD need to do to become a "must-have", "desirable" function for Organisations? points out the following:*
>
> *The concept of Use of Self is a core one for OD. As many writers (Nevis, Seashore, Jamieson, Cheung-Judge, Burke) put it – Use of Self is the way in which we act upon our observations, values,*

feelings and then intentionally execute an intervention necessary for the situation that presents. As we develop a heightened self-awareness, we allow our own sensations, feelings, knowledge and judgement to inform what action (or no action) we will need to take.

(Jenkins, 2021, p. 64)

Some key points here therefore, as we consider the question *What can individuals do to manage or live with a toxic colleague* are:

- To encourage self-awareness in yourself,

- To encourage self-awareness in that colleague,

- To be brave and courageous in providing grounded feedback, and

- As evidenced by the sharing by the individuals in Chapter 5, to take care of yourself and your mental well-being through ensuring amongst other things that you have a tribe or a close confidante that you can rely on.

Self-awareness is key – and is going to be a challenge for many toxic leaders. Dr Tasha Eurich, an expert in self-awareness, provides some fascinating insights to help 'size' the challenge of enabling self-awareness to emerge in different types of people. Her research suggests that there are three types of people when it comes to understanding a person's openness to feedback (to help increase self-awareness). These are:

1. *Lost Causes* – people who have no self-knowledge and no motivation to acquire it;

2. *Aware Don't Care* – those who know the impact they are having and have no intention of changing – they usually think that their counterproductive and often borderline abusive behaviour is getting them what they want;

3. *The Nudgeable* – these are people who genuinely want to be better but they don't know how to change – and Dr Eurich suggests that an approach combining feedback with compassion can be very successful with this type of person.

(https://www.youtube.com/watch?app=desktop
&v=hpb1rCf5Jlo&feature=youtu.be)

From Dr Eurich's work, we can see that some people will be open to feedback, perhaps delivered through a coaching interaction – whereas others will be resolutely resistant to such feedback. Some might say these 'feedback-resistant' people are 'uncoachable'. To understand more about this, I took the opportunity to ask an India-based coach, Shruti Swaroop, about the 'coachability' of people we might regard as displaying toxic or dysfunctional behaviour and asked her whether she thought some people were uncoachable. Here's what Shruti said:

> Some people need intensive counselling and coaching. And I mean intensive. Many have found that the various therapies they've tried haven't worked – which suggests that things are deeply wrong. Are people "uncoachable"? Well, I have had few – well, three. I've seen people reach out when they can't find answers themselves. Then when they start to figure it out, they often don't realise that is the coach who has helped them to get to where they are! And it's at that point that they say: Oh, I didn't think I need a coach anyway – and off they go!

It is clear that behavioural change is really difficult to achieve unless the person wants to change. As Dr Eurich mentioned about the 'Nudgeables' – many people need help understanding *how to go about trying to change* – and that is where coaching can clearly play a valuable role.

BOARDS

Earlier in *Toxic Humans*, I made the point that Boards need to be safe spaces in which healthy debate and the ability to dissent can coexist alongside warm and authentic support. I think it is also incumbent on – and is a real challenge to some Chairs – for Chairs to be able to discern between truly toxic behaviour and behaviour that *appears toxic to some people*. It's necessary for us to accept that different people have different tolerance levels for toxicity and it is this sensitivity to nuance that I think Chairs need to be aware of and – if they feel they need to work on this more – to invest time and effort in studying what makes people behave in the way that they do.

It's also important to recognise that toxic behaviour can arise as a result of an individual's back story which may not be apparent to everyone or even shared by the individual: for this reason, we need to take an informed, cautious and empathetic approach to implementing some of the Antidote Actions that I suggest below.

As Adarsh Mantravadi shares:

> Difficult board members do crop up. The reasons why may be obvious or creep up overtime. They frequently miss board or committee meetings or show up completely unprepared. They display antagonism towards staff or disrupt meetings with a toxic attitude; they lack sufficient financial literacy to help make informed business decisions, or they are staunchly opposed to using new technology when preparing for a board meeting.
>
> More subtle signs might involve a board member getting burned out over time, becoming distracted by personal issues, or participating more passively in board meetings with the simple "go along to get along" approach to performing their duties.
>
> In either case a difficult board member can personally affect the board's productivity and decision-making efforts, and ultimately cost your entire organisation time and money.
>
> (Mantravadi, The Center for Association Leadership, 2023)

A.J. Sidransky provides us with a build on the perspective of Adarsh Mantravani:

> When a board is burdened with individuals who cannot - or will not - get along with the rest of the board, or who consistently have their own agenda that conflicts with the priorities of the rest of the board and the community as a whole, it can be difficult if not possible to govern effectively.
>
> There are many effects of toxic behaviour on governance….but all have one thing in common: toxic board members prevent the board of directors from performing their fiduciary duty for the community by creating unnecessary distractions. Because they often involve

extraneous issues unrelated to the goals of the community, the results can impede the board's decision-making process.

(Sidransky, 2022)

And Boardroom psychologist Rob Newman has this to share:

A bad behaviour such as dominating by the Chair triggers a reaction such as anxiety or silence in other directors, and when this reciprocating pattern repeats over time, a habit is formed in the group which leeches into and shapes boardroom culture. But if you can catch bad behaviour early then you can prevent it from becoming a habitual boardroom dynamic that affects group discussion and decision making.
   – Rob Newman quoted by Shelley Dempsey, Dealing with toxic behaviour in the boardroom, Australian Institute of Company Directors, article on the website Dealing with toxic behaviour in the boardroom (aicd.com.au)

Rob Newman believes that groupthink or the creation of a climate of distrust and conflict often occur as a result of the build-up of bad behaviours from individual directors – bad behaviours that have gone unaddressed. In Table 6, we can see some of the issues associated with toxicity that a Chair of a Board might have to deal with. These are things that the Chair would need to address as soon as possible, rather than taking a 'wait and see' approach and hoping things will somehow get better (in my experience, they don't) and as per the old adage 'Hope is Not a Strategy' (Michael E. Porter) – it is incumbent on us to take action. Naturally, this needs to happen after careful and thoughtful analysis of the presenting issue.

Table 6. For Your Toolkit – 8 Antidote Actions for Boards.

Issue	Antidote
1 Poor conduct	Consistent enforcement of an agreed Code of Conduct where everyone has an opportunity to speak, and mutual respect and civility are expected
2 Unacceptable remarks as part of poor behaviour	Call this out immediately. Don't ignore it. When something awkward or untoward has been said during the board meeting, catch up with your colleague to share with

(Continued)

Table 6. (Continued)

Issue	Antidote
	them in more detail what you heard and how it made you feel. Ask them for their take on the same incident. Make sure that they understand the impact they are having
3 Conflicts of interest	Members should recuse themselves
4 Emergence of a toxic board member	Don't ignore it: acknowledge and address the problem – open up dialogue with the person and create a plan for action
5 Consistent lack of preparation	The Chair must take the issue offline with the individual to find out what is preventing the person from preparing appropriately for the board meetings – and offer support and counsel to help solve the issue. There might be a need to reshape the information supplied or to provide it even further ahead of time
6 A board member presents as a troublemaker	Is it the case that they are a bona fide troublemaker or is it really just well-intentioned dissent? The Chair should not try to shut down such a person but seek to understand their style and motivations better
7 A sense that the Board is not functioning as well as it could be – a hint of toxicity is in the air	Conduct Board peer reviews to establish how people feel about their own performance as well as others – enlist the support of the governance committee to get this off the ground
8 Consistently toxic board member	Take action to remove them according to the guidelines and protocols which govern the action of the Board

Table inspired by and with thanks to Adarsh Mantravani and A.J. Sidransky, created by the author.

And finally:

The most involved, diligent, value-adding boards create a virtuous cycle in which the good qualities of one board member build upon another. They develop trust and mutual respect, and they challenge each other by asking intelligent questions in a spirited give-and-take environment.

(Mantravadi, The Center for Association Leadership, 2021)

I think this is an excellent observation and I am particularly taken by the notion of the creation of a 'virtuous cycle' whereby 'the good qualities of one board member build upon another'. I think this has got to be one of the most potent antidotes to toxic humans in Boards. The other is to ensure that cohesion of the Board is made a top priority. As Annette Templeton points out in an article in Psychology Today:

> *Effective governance requires that the board functions as a cohesive entity versus a loosely connected group of experts. Ensure that the board has a regular cadence and a clear set of guiding principles for governing together: being explicitly aligned around an action plan if an ethical concern arises with the company's leadership is essential to truly fulfilling board duties. One example of where boards misstep is inconsistent meeting practices and varying levels of relationship with the CEO. This undermines the leverage to intervene when bad behaviour emerges.*
> – Annette Templeton, Boards must intervene to end toxic behaviour in the C-suite – Destructive leadership extracts organisational costs that boards cannot ignore.

And one of the leading thinkers on effective Board functioning has this to say:

> *Respect and trust do not imply endless affability or absence of disagreement. Rather, they imply bonds among board members that are strong enough to withstand clashing viewpoints and challenging questions.*
> (Sonnenfeld, 2002)

SENIOR TEAMS

There is a vast body of literature and research about the workings of teams – as well as how to manage problem areas and to lead teams effectively. So the list of issues and their possible 'antidotes' that I share below is not intended to be exhaustive: it is a distillation of some 'big ticket' negative factors that I have observed over many years working as part of a team, leading a team, interpreting (Japanese and English) for teams and facilitating teams (as part of a programme, workshop or seminar on leadership development). Cumulatively, these negative factors create an atmosphere of stress and anxiety that damages mental well-being and of course, performance. The Antidotes I propose below should be seen a jumping off point for discussion.

Everyone is different and every situation has its own nuances and idio-
syncrasies. Nowhere is this more apparent than in different country cultures.
Friends and colleagues across Asia and the Middle East have remarked upon
the role of hierarchy in Asian and Middle Eastern corporate cultures: it can be
next to impossible in some environments to even come close to being able to
challenge the boss about anything! In these situations it is going to be even
more important to have a close confidante or a supportive group of friends to
help you get through the worst patches. My sense is that change is going to be
slow in highly hierarchical societies primarily because the genesis for the
toxicity that people experience lower down in the organisation *is at the top*.
This toxic behaviour is condoned by the people in power and supported
through systemic toxic collusion (often manifested by an inability – or lack of
motivation – to speak up and speak out). See Table 7.

Table 7. For Your Toolkit – 8 Antidote Actions for Senior Teams.

Issue	Antidote
1 Passive–aggressive behaviour	Passive–aggressive behaviour shows up in a multiplicity of ways ranging from questioning a suggestion you've made: 'Really? When we tried that before it didn't work, but if you want to have another go – well, *you're the boss*!' to feigning vagueness or ignorance when everyone knows the truth of the matter: 'Oh, I thought we discussed that before and decided not to go ahead? Maybe I misheard you'. Persistent under-mining of a colleague in this way is truly draining: it exhausts everyone except the passive-aggressor (who is probably enjoying the awkwardness he or she is creating). It needs to be called out and discussed.
2 Persistent naysaying	'That won't work'. I think we have all heard colleagues saying this and depending on the context, it might be a reasonable opinion to share. But relentless naysaying and cynicism is different: it is another source of stress (particularly for the leader of the team) and it is a matter of urgency that this behaviour is challenged. That said, replying to the naysayer with a challenge back: 'Well, what would you suggest?' is likely to result in a 'Well I don't know, but I know that [what you are proposing] won't work'. You will have to get to the bottom of this: try to find out the root cause by having a one-to-one with the person.
3 Incivility	An example of incivility is when a team member uses an expletive which is wholly inappropriate to the situation. Some habitual users of the 'f-word' use it deliberately to create tension and put people off-balance. We should be brave and

Table 7. (Continued)

Issue	Antidote
	say: Please don't use that kind of language. Sometimes using the f-word or similar can be acceptable but making a habit of it shows contempt for group norms and civility.
4 Blaming	'I don't know what happened there, but if you ask me, [name of another person] is probably responsible'. People generally avoid blaming because it never ends well, but *in extremis* and when the team is falling short, it is often the case that team members will look for a scapegoat. We should vigorously challenge such behaviour and ask the person making the assertion (as to who is to blame) to give details and specifics.
5 Bullying	Bullying or intimidating behaviour, especially by bosses – but by no means limited to them – can take many forms. Encroaching on people's personal space by thrusting your jaw out, neck forwards into their face while saying, in response to an answer the person has given: 'That is a good answer but *it's not the answer to my question*. Let me ask you again [repeats question]' is one example of such bullying behaviour. In many cases the person doing the bullying isn't fully aware of the effect their words and body language are having. So a conversation away from the meeting to challenge the person with the bullying behaviour – should be the next action. If you are made anxious or even frightened by the thought of having that sort of conversation, talk it over with a close friend or confidante and decide how you are going to conduct the discussion. If you have a coach, discuss your strategy with them.
6 Conflict avoidance	Creative tension in teams is something that is incredibly powerful – and necessary. Robust debate plus good-natured disagreement is an excellent pathway to achieving a good outcome for a plan or a project. But when a team is dysfunctional, perhaps as a result of a domineering leader or because of the 'below the radar' interaction of sub-cliques within the bigger team – the outcome can be disastrous. So avoiding conflict by deciding not to share your opinion or ideas and simply staying silent – is also poisonous for teams. In Japanese culture (and this holds true for Japanese business culture), the practice of silence – of 'freezing people out' by more or less ignoring them – is a favoured way to show contempt, dislike or hatred for someone or something – without actually saying a word. This is also a good example of extreme passive–aggressive behaviour.
7 Distrust	The issues 1–6 are deadly for effective team working because they destroy trust. And building trust is one of the most challenging things that a leader needs to do. I believe that leaders cannot *make* people trust them, or each other – but

(Continued)

Table 7. (Continued)

Issue	Antidote
	what they can do is to create an atmosphere within which trust can start to develop. That means increasing credibility (yours, as a leader), being seen as reliable ('say what you'll do, do what you say') developing 'intimacy', i.e. warm interpersonal relationships and very importantly, minimising what is known as 'self-orientation' or the tendency to see the world only from your point of view. Check out the Trust Equation which was conceived by David Maister and launched in 2000. It is explained in detail by TrustedAdvisor Associates LLC https://trustedadvisor.com/why-trust-matters/understanding-trust/understanding-the-trust-equation
8 Lack of safety	A great deal has been written about the importance of psychological safety by great scholars such as Amy Edmondson of Harvard – and it really cannot be underestimated. I also like the contribution made by the Canadian thinker Gervase Bushe in his whitepaper *Most of the Advice About Psychological Safety at Work Isn't Helpful*, who says this: 'To create a psychologically safe environment you have to expect that everyone will be experiencing things differently from you, and be curious about what people's experience really is. Sometimes that will make you uncomfortable – but it's not them who are making you uncomfortable – it's you who makes you uncomfortable. You are responsible for your own experience. If you make others responsible for your discomfort, they will get that message and will learn what not to say around you'. (Gervase Bushe, Most of the Advice About Psychological Safety at Work Isn't Helpful)

ISSUES IN OTHER WORK CONTEXTS – WHETHER IN HIERARCHICAL, HOLACRATIC OR START-UP STRUCTURES

In 2022, the staff of the Museum of Fine Arts in Brussels wrote in an open letter to Thomas Dermine, the Secretary of State in charge of federal museums in Belgium, to complain that they were employed under 'appalling working conditions'. Earlier reports in the Belgian Francophone press had made mention of the 'toxic' working climate (le climat de travail 'toxique').

https://www.rtbf.be/article/nouvelles-plaintes-aux-musees-royaux-des-beaux-arts-on-a-peut-etre-trop-peu-soigne-les-conditions-de-travail-reagit-le-directeur-11139248

Interestingly, complaints were also raised about the integration (or lack thereof) of young people due the *structural* nature of the museum's organisation:

> It is perhaps the problem of a very hierarchical, very vertical struc-
> ture, [plus] an administration [addressing].... the aspirations of a
> younger generation with expectations that do not correspond to a
> very pyramidal vision like that practiced by the museum.
>
> –https://www.rtbf.be/article/des-conditions-de-travail-
> epouvantables-des-employes-du-musee-des-beaux-arts-de-brux-
> elles-pointent-du-doigt-leur-directeur-michel-draguet-11124231

Connecting structure to culture and generational difference and then connecting it to organisational toxicity – is a fascinating link to make. This concerns the discipline of Organisational Design (OD) – which means that it (OD) – given that it is clearly something that we can (usually) influence and change – offers some scope for us to look at how we can design organisations to foster collaboration and address generational expectations (for more democratic and consultative working for example) and thereby to minimise the potential for toxicity to arise (from a structure that isn't fit for purpose).

So while structure influences organisational culture and may cause toxicity if not done right, there are some other issues facing us which I would like to share here in Table 8, along with some suggested 'antidotes'.

Table 8. For Your Toolkit – 10 Antidote Actions for General Organisational Contexts.

	Issue	Antidote
1	Frustration with the structure of the organisation	All organisations have a shape (typically, 'diamond-shaped' or 'Christmas Tree-shaped'. Some are inverted pyramids). Most have tended to be variations on the classic pyramidal structure. As we look into the future, these traditional structures are being augmented by flatter structures as well as more dispersed structures (such as the DAOs or Decentralised Autonomous Organisations). Matching the structure to the people and the people to the structure may offer some scope to better manage expectations and reduce the potential for stress-induced toxicity (as we saw in the Museum of Fine Arts example above). It is also important to

(Continued)

Table 8. (Continued)

Issue	Antidote
	realise that it is not so much a case of 'flat = good, hierarchy = bad' – but more a question of what is appropriate for the stage of evolution of that particular organisation, what kind of culture you are trying to foster and what kind of business and employee needs are you trying to meet. I have met start-ups that had a 'family atmosphere' that seemed to be right for the early stages of the business but over time – and with tremendous success and a rapidly growing workforce – things change. Sometimes these organisations will come to you to say: We need structure! We need to contain the chaos! Help!
2 Frustration with the nature of job and work design	Think about reviewing your jobs and 'job families'. Explore whether there is a way to streamline things to reduce redundancy of time and effort so as to reduce the levels of stress and anxiety that people feel. Deploy job and work design techniques such as *Uncoupling* (where you split one role into two new jobs at the same level), *Unstacking* (separating tasks into two new jobs at different levels and *Segmenting* (taking portions out of several jobs and re-assembling them into brand new jobs). You can also consider enlarging a person's job to make it more challenging (Job Enlargement), or enriching someone's job to make it more exciting (Job Enrichment). These are all positive actions which can take the sting out of some jobs that lack challenge, cause boredom and create tension, potentially leading to the development of a toxic vibe in the workplace ('Idle hands are the devil's workshop').
3 Intergenerational tensions	Intergenerational tensions are nothing new. In recent years the discourse has been about how to manage the millennials – but that's now changed to discussion about how millennial management needs to manage other generations – how they should interact with Gen Z, for example – and that's even *before* we start getting ready for the arrival of Gen Alpha! One way to defuse intergenerational tensions is to look for ways to improve communication channels. Many companies are using internal apps not only to facilitate communication between employees and the management but also between employees themselves. These apps are designed in a fun, creative and interesting way which helps to

Table 8. (Continued)

Issue	Antidote
	strengthen that feeling of being part of a bigger community. I have also noticed that learning and development professionals who involve the younger generation in the development of leadership development initiatives for that demographic – report high levels of engagement when they actually come to run the programmes. This should not come as a surprise because people have been actively invited to be involved in the creation of something. Nevertheless, it is all too often the case that even with the best of intentions, organisations end up 'doing things to people' when we all know that people don't like 'things being done to them'. Active involvement is a great antidote to toxicity.
4 Intercultural misunderstanding	Discord can arise in teams that are dispersed across many geographies and/or composed of people from many different cultural and language traditions. This discord can lead to toxicity unless efforts are made to bridge the gap to help people to gain a better perspective on how their colleagues see the work and to better understand the differences in how people communicate. The good news is that there are a number of skilled entities and individuals working in the intercultural communication space who can help. Help can come in the form of intercultural workshops using specialist psychometrics to generate data that can be used to unpick and understand the genesis of the discord. These workshops and support services are also beneficial in helping teams that are working pretty well – to work even better. So it is not always a remedial context within which progress can be made. One leading example is WorldWork, a company with a variety of tools available to help groups and teams that are working in an international context https://worldwork.global/
5 Empathy and compassion-free zones	Progress has been made in recent years to bring the idea of empathy and compassion into the workplace and to establish them as essential elements of good, human and effective leadership and management. Now, with the advance of AI, we are seeing tech helping with human emotion and assisting in the 'operationalisation' of empathy and compassion at work. One example of this is Warmspace https://warmspace.io/

(Continued)

Table 8. (Continued)

Issue	Antidote
	Warmspace 'invigorates teams through...tech-enabled guided interactions....when you use Warmspace technology, you're bringing the power of a top-tier organisational health consultant into every meeting, from the top executives to the individual contributors'. One application of Warmspace involves adopting (across the enterprise, for everyone) a daily routine or protocol conducted via one's mobile phone (or done in person) where you ask the other person to rate their mood at the beginning of the interaction and at the end: in between you ask each other: 'How are you?' And then 'How are you, *really*?' Pioneers like Patrick Cowden of The Beyond Company have enabled spectacular results from early adopters in traditionally 'tough' industries like brick manufacturing, providing a great example of operationalised 'empathy in action' and 'empathy at scale' – with all of it beautifully enabled by technology!
	Another exciting tech platform is Mursion https://www.mursion.com/ which uses 'human-powered AI' to master skills that drive performance by combining expertise in robotics, business analytics, project management and theatre to 'harness the best in artificial and human intelligence'.
	Then there is SoundWave https://www.soundwave.global/, which provides 'data-driven insights into how you talk, listen and are being heard and perceived by others....SoundWave looks at the way we use language and our conversational style, and demonstrates how – with intention and awareness – we can create meaningful relationships'.
6 Hidden Toxicity – so where *are* the toxic humans?	Sometimes organisations can labour under a general malaise characterised by low energy and a 'job's worth attitude' where people do the minimum required, avoid any initiative-taking and shirk responsibility. Where does this come from? It is likely to occur as a result of a combination of things: lack of purpose and vision, feelings of inequality and helplessness, uncaring and unhearing managers and a range of other negative factors. It could also come from subversive elements in the organisation too: people who often do not have positional power but wield a great deal of influence in their area. One way of identifying how people are connected in an organisation is to use Organisational

Table 8. (Continued)

Issue	Antidote
	Network Analysis (ONA) which is usually deployed for organisational design purposes to help planners figure out the people affiliations in organisations as part of project planning or strategic workforce planning. Such an analysis can shed light on who is allied with whom, who's an outlier, who has extensive people networks, the quality of those networks and so on. If certain connections are expected to be in place – but the data shows they are not – this would enable planners (in HR for example) to ask why. And in some cases, toxicity might be the cause – disrupting human connections that enable the organisation to function successfully. Another route to market is through 'HR Analytics' whereby we can use sophisticated tools (highly flexible employee engagement data derived from surveys of the workforce) – to look for signs that things are not working well (from a human/leadership perspective) in a particular part or parts of the organisation. This in turn allows the leadership of the organisation to prioritise and channel any interventions deemed necessary.
7 Toxic and Bullying Behaviour by Direct Reports	At a recent virtual seminar on bullying in the workplace (I went along out of curiosity), a straw poll of the online participants revealed that most people saw bullying as being something done by a manager to a subordinate. However, some people reported being bullied by their juniors – a situation others found hard to believe. And yet it most certainly happens: the person who was passed over to become boss (and now you're the boss, having previously been colleagues), questioning your ways of working, the undermining person who disputes (in a passive–aggressive way) every decision you make, the person who attempts to build a coalition of like-minded people to challenge your authority. Such situations demand action (not hope – i.e. hoping the problem will go away by itself – it never does). Follow due process, have honest one-to-ones, document the interactions, take advice from HR or your boss – and see where that takes you. If the answer is 'nowhere' – then move fast to exit the person.
8 Systemic Toxic Collusion (STC)	As we have noted at various points in *Toxic Humans*, STC is a very real issue. Turning a blind eye when someone is being bullied; failing to stand

(Continued)

Table 8. (Continued)

Issue	Antidote
	up for a colleague when they are being unfairly attacked; pretending not to notice discrimination; playing favourites or ignoring people's requests – and sometimes pleas – for support in withstanding pressure from a toxic leader or manager – these are just some of the manifestations of STC. Tackling STC will require leadership to create the conditions for, plus the promotion of, a culture of respect, civility and trust. It means going back to basics to build trust and ensure ethical behaviour. Leadership development, coaching and mentoring can play a part in supporting this – but it's really the leadership in the Board and the Senior Management Team that sets the tone – and that sets the organisation up for success or failure.
9 Leverage employee surveys	Make it safe for employees to provide the kind of feedback that will be useful to you and the organisation. Pay particular attention to the free-text responses. Then be sure to take action on that feedback. Try to check in with people to see whether their perception of the action you are taking maps with yours, or whether expectations are falling short (and you are unaware of this). Do as much benchmarking against other organisations to see how yours compares – and also, cherry-pick ideas that you think could work for your context.
10 Beware micro-cultures and pockets of toxicity	Try to measure your micro-cultures at a granular level: ask about and then attempt to measure sub-cultures created by individual leaders. We should encourage groups to define their own social norms (how they will work together) while at the same time promoting ideas of consistency and equality with other parts of the organisation or business so that the organisation *in toto* can move in one direction.

Let's now move on to Chapter 10 to reflect on what has been shared so far in *Toxic Humans* – and consider some further next steps to combatting poisonous leadership in Boards and senior teams.

10

REFLECTIONS ON WHAT TOXIC HUMANS, UNCHECKED, CAN DO TO ORGANISATIONS – AND HOW TO CONTAIN OR STOP THEM

At the beginning of *Toxic Humans*, we took a brief look at the history of toxic humans in popular culture while also examining some of the historical, larger than life, controversial figures in business who exhibited what we might broadly describe as toxic behaviour and who met, to a greater or lesser extent, the litmus tests or definitions of toxicity as proposed by Marcia Lynn Whicker, Jean Lipman-Blumen, Carol Dweck, Martha Stout, John A. Byrne, Simon Baron-Cohen, Jon Ronson, Robert Hart and Dr Mark Freestone. We started to uncover the factors that appear to come together, like the human equivalent of a perfect storm, to produce people who manage to leave an indelible imprint in the memories of those with whom they interacted, as well as an often long-lasting and profound effect on those organisations which, in many cases, they played a lead role in destroying.

We took some time to ponder the question of toxicity in leaders of organisations by exploring the deeper recesses of the human psyche and the inner workings of psychopaths and narcissists. As we delved deeper into the focus areas of Boards and Senior Management teams, we started to look for patterns, and I proposed a set of personas to help identify common behaviours of toxic members of such teams or groups as a starting point for figuring out a way to understand them – and to live and work alongside them. Much has been written in recent years about the importance of psychological safety (PS) in organisations, and so we looked at how toxic or dysfunctional personalities negatively impact PS, bringing a whole host of issues that destroy value and – critically – lives.

Throughout the book, we have noted that while certain antisocial or disruptive behaviour would qualify as toxic for some people, for others it is simply a manifestation of a certain kind of leadership style. This difference in perception is important because even as we recognise different realities, there is a line which when crossed is *for most people* a red line which they will confidently describe as the moment of entering a zone of toxicity. The recollections from interviews with people who have worked with toxic bosses and individuals across many different sectors and across the globe show that most people can discern irregularity and abnormal behaviour when it reaches certain levels of intensity and often depravity. For this reason, I decided to present toxicity through the lens of differing degrees of a lack of affective empathy, connecting this to work done on understanding evil as depicted in the work of Simon Baron-Cohen. I called this the Empathy-Toxicity Spectrum. In the interviews conducted with a diverse group of people, I was also keen to find out what coping strategies my interviewees developed to manage their lives in the shadow of a toxic Board member or senior leader. These ranged from resigning, to drawing on the supportive power of their female networks (in the case of women subjected to toxic pressure by predominantly male leaders) to taking legal action as the only possible recourse. And as we heard about the often breathtakingly nefarious behaviours of toxic leaders, we also paused to consider the impact of early childhood experiences in shaping people as adults and the significance of people having a secure base as they grow up, positing at the same time the idea that given their often appalling experiences as young people, 'toxic leaders' are deeply deserving of our compassion and empathy.

We then moved on to consider how and when toxicity in organisations might emerge, using the employee lifecycle as a framework to understand this and from there, how we might evolve ways to circumvent the very emergence of toxicity, in order to mitigate it and manage it. Possible future countermeasures point to the potential for artificial intelligence (AI) to help us to dampen toxicity – and enable people to develop their resilience in order to coexist with toxicity. Some of these uplifting tech-based solutions are already with us or evolving quickly. This has to be cause for some joy! The final chapters of *Toxic Humans* contain a number of toolkits for Boards, for

Senior Management teams and for other organisational contexts – repositories of possible actions to take and resources upon which to draw.

FURTHER CONSIDERATIONS

In *Toxic Humans*, I have suggested a simple conceptual equation for thinking about how toxic humans come to be.

The Toxicity Equation©:

Toxicity in Humans at Work = Genetic Predisposition + Environmental Shaping* − Empathy + Work Context + Systemic Collusion

*childhood upbringing

While this alone does not provide any easy answers as to how we deal with toxicity in Boards and Organisations more broadly, it does give us some starting points as we try to make sense of the behaviour of those individuals who manage to visit so much pain and stress on people in the workplace. It also helps us to prioritise *where* to help such people – if indeed we can help them. It is clear that our response to many people with dysfunctional behaviour should be one of understanding and compassion.

We cannot do much about genetic disposition or childhood upbringing (although we can try to show understanding for those who have had a rough early life). I think we can do a lot to dial up our empathy (affective empathy is emphasised here), and there is a lot of scope to positively affect (to the degree we can) – the work context (although this might be very difficult to do) and to challenge Systemic Toxic Collusion (STC) – also a tough issue to tackle.

In some of our stories of people's experience of toxic humans, many of the toxic people depicted in our stories did what they did because they had the power to abuse: sometimes they did what they did simply because they derived pleasure from inflicting pain and suffering.

This is why I think that we have a lot of scope to do better, particularly in the area of recruitment of non-toxic people into organisations – and on to Boards too.

In my earlier book *Expert Humans*, I introduced a simple model called Altruism, Compassion and Empathy (ACE) and suggested that applying these human qualities to tackle some of our most pressing issues as members of the human race – namely sustainability, digital transformation, inequality, global human health and trust (that is, the crisis in trust across the world) – might just be part of the answer or at least part of the response we need to make to address these immense issues. Thanks to the efforts of many thinkers and influencers around the world such as Brené Brown, Kristen Neff and others, empathy has entered our business and management lexicon. This is a positive development. But there is still more that needs to be done because empathy is only part of the story: the true destination is compassion: compassionate action and compassionate leadership. Organisations such as the Stanford Center for Compassion and Altruism Research and Education (CCARE) at https://ccare.stanford.edu/ and the recently formed Global Compassion Coalition at https://global-compassioncoalition.org/ – are making great strides to make compassion in the global workplace as accessible and as mainstream an idea as empathy. But even as we agitate for more compassion and empathy, I also think we need to be more assertive about identifying toxicity and calling it out.

In this book, the focus has been on Boards and Organisations and within this, the senior people in organisations because it is with these groups that role-modelling, purpose-setting and championing values lie. As we have recognised already in *Toxic Humans*, toxicity in organisations has a nasty habit of starting at the top and percolating down. People I spoke to sometimes recalled (in horror) the realisation that the toxicity they themselves experienced had actually started to *seep into their own human interactions with their own teams and colleagues* – proof positive (if you like) of the insidious nature of toxicity, spreading poison into the heart of the organisation and the hearts of working people. This is where I see the existence of 'systemic toxic collusion' come into play – the phenomenon by which toxic leaders manage to do what they do, reaching dizzying heights in organisations. We observe their rise with a mixture of incredulity and despair: how, we ask ourselves, did they manage to get there?

I think the answer lies partly with the toxic humans themselves, of course (and their often astounding ability to 'manage up') – but I think it is also something that is aided and abetted by people consciously or unconsciously colluding with the toxic leader (sometimes driven by fear, or simply through indifference or lack of attention, until it is too late). It may be useful to think of all of these things as being part of the 'Toxic Triangle' we met in Chapter 9 – the three corners of the triangle represented by destructive leaders, susceptible followers and conducive environments.

The Way Forward

(A) *Antidote Actions* – Combatting poisonous leadership in Boards and Organisations is going to take concerted effort and a great deal of courage. I am cheered by the bravery of the people I spoke to for this book and the stories of others uncovered through my research. I think we need to embrace the light, positive side – of altruism, compassion and empathy – while at the same time confronting the dark, negative side, namely the toxicity prevalent in the workplace and the toxic humans we find there. I think we have to be clear on the values we are looking to live by – this is vital and obvious – but at the same time, we need to do a much better job about stating what is acceptable and what we cannot and will not, as responsible and caring humans, tolerate.

(B) *Build Better Boards* – Progress is being made all the time to build better Boards – but there is still much to do. We need to press for improved Board accountability in many geographies and encourage more self-reflection by Board members. We should press Boards to not only provide oversight of organisational culture but to take a more active yet nuanced role in helping to shape that culture. They should get involved in exercises and activities that look at values and behaviours in the organisation and bring their consider-able experience and insights to bear – again in a supportive rather than directive manner. A good balance of support and challenge is what is required to help organisations be true to their people and to their purpose, vision and mission. We should encourage more thoughtfulness and care around Board composition, i.e. be mindful of who is being brought in.

What's the Value That People Bring and What's the Purpose of the Board?

In my conversation with Sandra Guerra, a deeply experienced Board member, co-founder of Better Governance, based in São Paulo, Brazil and author of *The Black Box of Governance,* Sandra made the point that fundamental to the question of who is brought onto a Board is: *What value is this person likely to bring to the organisation?* That has got to be the genesis for everything. Helle Bank Jørgensen, the CEO of Competent Boards, based in Canada, agrees, sharing that 'we have to do our due diligence on all Board members. It's not a question of "Do I like this person" but much more "Do I believe that this person can *give* something to the organisation?" Helle went on to tell me that we need to ask, "What is the purpose of the Board?" – and to be able to have a truly rich discussion about that, Helle adds, "We need to have foresight" – which is where the Board Skills Matrix comes in. As Helle says: "If we're planning to sell products and services in Asia but I have no one on the Board, who has any knowledge of doing that in Asia, how then do I get that insight? Is there another way to get to this? We need to do our homework, we need to ask, "What's missing?" and if we think we need to build the capacity to think differently, then we need to address that honestly as well."'

The Board Skills Matrix

A Board will task a small group of people to create a Board Skills Matrix which can then be used to surface any gaps in the Board's knowledge or skills. This will inform any future plans for adding new people to the Board – in other words, bringing in new people with the skills and knowledge that might be lacking in the existing group of members. After all, as Sandra Guerra points out, Boards are all about moving from a 'controlled ownership' to a 'shared ownership'. Sandra also shared that the Board Skills Matrix approach used by a number of organisations has not traditionally factored in human skills (such as empathy and compassion) at all (when in fact, they should). Related to this, a Chair who is involved in face-to-face interviews with candidates for the Board must be *equipped* to ask the right kinds of questions: they must also be able to assess the candidate's reaction to those (often deliberately) very direct questions. As Helle shared with me, a great deal of responsibility lies on the shoulders of the Chair for managing the human dynamics in Boards – 'you're dealing with "super-smart people" with their own ideas, who have grown up in a certain way, maybe having had to struggle to get ahead, often against the odds – elbowing their way up in some cases – only to find themselves in a team situation for which they aren't always well-prepared'. And it's the role of the Chair to manage all the different views and to promote the idea that no question is a dumb question. As Helle said, so insightfully, 'The Chair needs to ensure no stone is left unturned' – and at the same time be crystal-clear with the Board members that: 'You don't get to throw any stones!'

Come by More Often

I was reminded of the fact that Board members are often relatively infrequent visitors to the organisations they serve as directors, and Sandra suggested that it would be ideal if the normal 'cadence' (meeting frequency) of the Board could be increased from the typical four times a year to eight times a year (in countries like Brazil it is common for Boards to meet around 10 times a year and in some cases, even twelve times a year). This would afford the Board members the opportunity to better understand the culture of the company and to help shape it – which strikes me as a great idea.

Ongoing Development for Board Members

We're lucky that there are some excellent options for Board Members to develop their skills. Various programmes are offered by the following organisations which are well-worth looking into (this is a non-exhaustive listing):

- Australian Institute of Company Directors – Company Directors course;

- Competent Boards – Corporate Board Training Programmes;

- Financial Times Board Programmes – FT Non-Executive Director Diploma;

- Henley Business School – Certificate in Board Practice and Directorship;

- INSEAD – International Directors Programme;

- SusteneriGroup – Board Directors programmes;

- Virtual Advisory Board Programmes for Boards – various workshops and seminars.

It's really encouraging that such organisations are working hard to Build Better Boards.

(C) *Compassion With Teeth* – Finally, I think we need what I would call 'compassion with teeth'.

What I mean by this is that we need to continue to push the compassion (and empathy) agenda *but at the same time* challenge ourselves hard to tackle toxicity head-on: to encourage people to say: 'This is not acceptable' and to implement tougher measures on people who display the kind of toxic behaviours that harm people and organisations. We need to combine compassion with toughness.

This means better screening, better people development and ultimately, better support for *all* the human beings in our workplaces.

In the final analysis, it means more ethical and caring leadership from those in positions of power – from those Board members and senior leaders who could make a real difference.

If they wanted to.

BIBLIOGRAPHY

AmericanRhetoric.com. (2018, January 7). *Richard Fuld – Lehman Brothers Bankruptcy testimony (enhanced audio)* [Video]. YouTube. https://www.youtube.com/watch?v=Mte6-u84Ehk

Baron-Cohen, S. (2011). *The science of evil: On empathy and the origins of cruelty.*

Bloom, P. (2018). *Against empathy: The case for rational compassion.* Vintage.

Bregman, P. (2021, February 1). Empathy starts with curiosity. *Harvard Business Review.* https://hbr.org/2020/04/empathy-starts-with-curiosity

Buckingham, L., & Kane, F. (2020, March 26). From the archive, 22 August 1992: Gerald Ratner's "crap" comment haunts jewellery chain. *The Guardian.* https://www.theguardian.com/business/2014/aug/22/gerald-ratner-jewellery-total-crap-1992-archive

Bushe, G. (n.d.). *Most of the advice about psychological safety at work isn't helpful.* https://b-m-institute.com/. https://b-m-institute.com/wp-content/uploads/2021/12/psychological_safety_whitepaper.pdf. Accessed on May 1, 2023.

Byrne, J. A. (2005, January 7). *Working for the boss from hell.* Fast Company.

Chamorro-Premuzic, T. (2012). The dark side of Charisma. *Harvard Business Review.*

Charan, R., Carey, D., & Useem, M. (2014). *Boards that lead: When to take charge, when to partner, and when to stay out of the way.* Harvard Business Review Press.

Chau, A., Zhong, W., Gordon, B., Krueger, F., & Grafman, J. (2018). Anterior insula lesions and alexithymia reduce the endorsements of everyday altruistic attitudes. *Neuropsychologia*, 117, 428–439. https://doi.org/10.1016/j.neuropsychologia.2018.07.002

CIPD | Selection Methods. (n.d.). CIPD. https://www.cipd.org/uk/knowledge/factsheets/selection-factsheet/

Cook, J. (2020, May 18). The 6 childhood trends of successful entrepreneurs. *Forbes.* https://www.forbes.com/sites/jodiecook/2020/05/18/childhood-trends-of-entrepreneurs/?sh=a29150d72e96

CultureX About Us. (n.d.). https://www.culturex.com/about-us

Dempsey, S., & Australian Institute of Company Directors. (n.d.). *Dealing with toxic behaviour in the boardroom – AICD.* https://www.aicd.com.au/organisational-culture/business-ethics/business-conduct/dealing-with-toxic-behaviour-in-the-boardroom.html

Dina. (2023, March 10). *Communication consulting tools for effective communication.* SoundWave – Building Skilful Dialogue. https://www.soundwave.global/

Dweck, C. S. (2016). *Mindset: The new psychology of success.* Ballantine Books. (Original work published 2006).

Edmondson, A. C. (2018). *The fearless organization: Creating psychological safety in the workplace for learning, innovation, and growth.* John Wiley & Sons.

EDSI. (2022, October 6). *Employer branding.* https://www.edsisolutions.com/solutions/employer-branding

Employee lifecycle: The 7 stages every employer must understand and improve. (2023, January 20). Qualtrics. https://www.qualtrics.com/experience-management/employee/employee-lifecycle/

Employer Branding. (2022, October 6). Educational Data Systems Inc. https://www.edsisolutions.com/solutions/employer-branding. Accessed on April 2, 2023.

Erikson, T. (2022). *Surrounded by Narcissists: Or, how to stop other people's egos ruining your life.* St. Martin's Essentials.

Eurich, T. (2017). *How to deal with delusional people* [Video]. https://www.youtube.com/watch?app=desktop&v=hpb1rCf5Jlo&feature=youtu.be

Excelsior. (2020, December 10). *The most toxic person in the workplace – by Simon Sinek* [Video]. YouTube. https://www.youtube.com/watch?v=ljLlpOAGRsQ

Feloni, R. (2016, November 18). *Richard Branson explains the most important lesson he learned from his mom — And it included being pushed out of the car at age 6.* Business Insider. https://www.businessinsider.com/richard-branson-mom-taught-him-take-risks-2016-11

Freestone, M. (2020). *Making a Psychopath: My journey into 7 dangerous minds.* Random House.

Gamba Quilliam, G. (2023). *CIPD | Talent Management | Factsheets.* https://www.cipd.org/uk/knowledge/factsheets/talent-factsheet/

Goyal, R., Kakabadse, N. K., Kakabadse, A., Moore, P. L., & Morais, F. (2017). *Conflict and tension in the boardroom: How managing disagreement improved board dynamics.* Henley Business School & ICSA Chartered Secretaries.

Graham, D. A. (2023, March 24). The most disturbing part of Trump's latest rant. *The Atlantic.* https://www.theatlantic.com/ideas/archive/2023/03/trumps-threats-death-and-destruction-if-indicted/673508/

Green, R. (2022). 10 most common psychometric tests: A list. *Practice Aptitude Tests.* https://www.practiceaptitudetests.com/resources/10-most-common-psychometric-tests/

Guerra, S. (2021). *The Black Box of Governance: Boards of directors revealed by those who inhabit them.* Routledge.

Haddad, D., & EdD CFRE. (n.d.). *Dysfunctional boards are the result of dysfunctional members.* LinkedIn. https://www.linkedin.com/pulse/dysfunctional-boards-result-members-duke-haddad-ed-d-cfre/?trk=articles_directory

Hired-gun CEO grew profits, fired thousands – Near Northwest. (n.d.). https://digitaledition.chicagotribune.com/tribune/article_popover.aspx?guid=eb84f245-1ba5-4d5c-a208-f9314127bd26

Isaac, G. (2013). The "toxic" director: It takes only one to derail the board. *Directors & Boards, 37*(5).

Isaac, A. (2023, April 24). CBI president says it failed to "filter out culturally toxic people" from ranks. https://www.theguardian.com/business/2023/apr/24/cbi-president-says-it-failed-to-filter-our-culturally-toxic-people-from-ranks

Istace, J. (2022). 'Des conditions de travail épouvantables': Des employés du Musée des Beaux-Arts de Bruxelles pointent du doigt leur directeur Michel Draguet. *RTBF.* https://www.rtbf.be/article/des-conditions-de-travail-epouvantables-des-employes-du-musee-des-beaux-arts-de-bruxelles-pointent-du-doigt-leur-directeur-michel-draguet-11124231

Jackson, C. (2023, January 4). 12 signs you're a super empath - relationships 101 - medium. Medium. https://medium.com/relationships101/12-signs-youre-a-super-empath-486376c69fc2

Jenkins, M. (2021). *Expert Humans: Critical leadership skills for a disrupted world.* Emerald Publishing Limited.

Johnston, J. E., & The Human Equation. (2011, April 27). Children who are cruel to animals: When to worry. *Psychology Today.*

Jones, O., & Bland, A. (2018, November 3). Philip Green allegations: "It's not banter, it's a climate of fear," claim staff. *The Guardian.* https://www.theguardian.com/business/2018/nov/02/philip-green-allegations-its-not-banter-its-a-climate-of-fear-say-staff

Knight, R. (2023, February 15). *How to be an empathetic boss, even when you're completely burned out.* Business Insider. https://www.businessinsider.com/ey-research-finds-americans-arent-getting-empathy-from-their-bosses-2021-10

Kouchaki, M., Leavitt, K., Zhu, L., & Klotz, A. C. (2023). Research: What fragile masculinity looks like at work. *Harvard Business Review.* https://hbr.org/2023/01/research-what-fragile-masculinity-looks-like-at-work

Leblanc, R., & Gillies, J. (2005). *Inside the boardroom: How boards really work and the coming revolution in corporate governance.* http://ci.nii.ac.jp/ncid/BA73499419

Levin, D. P. (1989). *Irreconcilable differences: Ross Perot versus General Motors.* Little, Brown and Company.

Lipman-Blumen, J. (2005, January/February). The allure of toxic leaders: Why followers rarely escape their clutches. *Ivey Business Journal*.

Lipman-Blumen, J. (2006). *The allure of toxic leaders: Why we follow destructive bosses and corrupt politicians—And how we can survive them*. Oxford University Press.

Loizos, C. (2018, May 2). *A CEO known publicly for the power of smiling was just ousted for intimidating employees*. TechCrunch.

Lu, D. (2023, February 15). Children will show compassion unless it costs them, research finds. *The Guardian*. https://www.theguardian.com/australia-news/2023/feb/16/children-will-show-compassion-unless-it-costs-them-research-finds

Mackintosh, T., & Manning, L., & BBC News. (n.d.). Met Police: Women and children failed by 'boys' club', review finds. https://www.bbc.com/news/uk-65015479. Accessed on March 21, 2023.

The Center for Association Leadership, & Mantravadi, A. (2023, May 8). *How to deal with bad board behavior*. ASAE. https://www.asaecenter.org/resources/articles/an_plus/2021/september/how-to-deal-with-bad-board-behavior

Martens, W. H. J., & W Kahn Institute of Theoretical Psychiatry and Neuroscience. (2008). Forensic psychiatry. *Medicine and Law*.

Martha Frick Sanger | C-SPAN.org. (1998, October 29). https://www.c-span.org/person/?57642/MarthaFrickSanger

Medland, D. (2016, July 16). U.K. Regulator gets serious on company culture and role of boards. *Fortune*.

Mitchell, K., & Waters, J., & BDO Australia. (2022). The 6 Bs of Talent Management: How to protect your competitive edge. www.bdo.com.au. https://www.bdo.com.au/en-au/insights/advisory/articles/the-6-bs-of-talent-management-how-to-protect-your-competitive-edge

Mursion. (2023, April 7). *Immersive learning simulations with human-powered AI | Mursion*. Virtual Reality Training Simulation Software by Mursion. https://www.mursion.com/

Nws, V. (2023, March 21). CEO van Plopsa moet opstappen na getuigenissen over "pestcultuur". *vrtnws.be*. https://www.vrt.be/vrtnws/nl/2023/03/20/studio-100-schuift-ceo-van-pretparkengroep-plopsa-steve-van-den/

Olgri, & Olgri. (2023). Nouvelles plaintes aux Musées royaux des Beaux-Arts: "On a peut-être trop peu soigné les conditions de travail", réagit le directeur. *RTBF*. https://www.rtbf.be/article/nouvelles-plaintes-aux-musees-royaux-des-beaux-arts-on-a-peut-etre-trop-peu-soigne-les-conditions-de-travail-reagit-le-directeur-11139248

Padilla, A., Hogan, R., & Kaiser, R. B. (2007). The toxic triangle: Destructive leaders, susceptible followers, and conducive environments. *The Leadership Quarterly*, *18*(3), 176–194. https://doi.org/10.1016/j.leaqua.2007.03.001

Panel, E. (2022, May 10). How to build a strong employer brand that attracts top talent. *Forbes*. https://www.forbes.com/sites/forbescommunicationscouncil/2022/05/10/how-to-build-a-strong-employer-brand-that-attracts-top-talent/?sh=32f58c472f99

Paulhus, D. L., & Williams, K. L. (2002). The dark triad of personality: Narcissism, Machiavellianism, and psychopathy. *Journal of Research in Personality*, 36(6), 556–563. https://doi.org/10.1016/s0092-6566(02)00505-6

Pernelet, H. R., & Brennan, N. (2022). Challenge in the boardroom: Director–manager question-and-answer interactions at board meetings. *Corporate Governance: An International Review*. https://doi.org/10.1111/corg.12492

PwC Governance Insights Center. (2020). *Turning crisis into opportunity: Pricewaterhouse coopers annual corporate directors survey 2020.*

Reich, C. (1985, April 21). The creative mind, the innovator. *New York Times Magazine*.

Ronson, J. (2011). *The psychopath test: A journey through the madness industry*. Pan Macmillan.

Ronson, J. (n.d.). *Strange answers to the psychopath test* [Video]. TED Talks. https://www.ted.com/talks/jon_ronson_strange_answers_to_the_psychopath_test?language=en

Sanger, M. F. S. (1998). *Henry Clay Frick: An intimate portrait*. Abbeville Publishing Group.

Scahill, L., & Kratochvil, C. (2010). *Pediatric psychopharmacology*. OUP.

Schlender, B., & Tetzeli, R. (2015). *Becoming Steve Jobs: The evolution of a reckless upstart into a visionary leader.*

Sidransky, A. J. (n.d.). *Dealing with the disruptive & disrespectful – Toxic board members*. New england condominium, the condo, HOA & Co-op monthly. https://newenglandcondo.com/article/toxic-board-members

Smith, H. (2019, January 28). Albert J. Dunlap, corporate turnaround specialist accused of accounting fraud, dies at 81. *The Washington Post*.

Smith Haghighi, A. (2021, July 6). What is the difference between sociopathy and psychopathy? *Medical News Today*.

Sonnenfeld, J. (1999, July). Carly Fiorina as a boss: The disappointing truth. *Fortune*.

Sonnenfeld, J. (2002). What makes great boards great. *Harvard Business Review*.

Sonnenfeld, J. A. (2014, August 1). What makes great boards great. *Harvard Business Review*. https://hbr.org/2002/09/what-makes-great-boards-great

Sports Direct treats workers "as commodities rather than human beings". (2016, July 22). SHP Safety and Health Practitioner.

Stern, S. (2009, September 22). Strengths become weaknesses. *The Financial Times*.

Sull, C. (2022). No leader can afford to ignore toxic culture. *Blog | CultureX*. https://blog.culturex.com/no-leader-can-afford-to-ignore-toxic-culture/

Sull, D. (2022, January 11). Toxic culture is driving the great resignation. *MIT Sloan Management Review*. https://sloanreview.mit.edu/article/toxic-culture-is-driving-the-great-resignation/

Sull, D., & Sull, C. (2022). How to fix a toxic culture. *MIT Sloan Management Review*. #64206.

Sull, D., & Sull, C. (2023). The toxic culture gap shows companies are failing women. *MIT Sloan Management Review*. #64407.

Sutton, R. (2007). Why I wrote the no asshole rule: Building a civilized workplace and surviving one that isn't. *Harvard Business Review*.

Taylor, A. (2013, April 3). History's 10 worst auto chiefs. *Fortune*.

Taylor, A., Erdman, A., Martin, J., & Walsh, T. (1992, November 16). U.S. cars come back. *Fortune*.

Team, M. (2020, June 15). The five dysfunctions of a team. *12min Blog*. https://blog.12min.com/the-five-dysfunctions-of-a-team-pdf/

Templeton, A. (2022). Boards must intervene to end toxic behaviour in the C-suite. *Psychology Today*.

The Economist. (2023a, February 23). Demands on corporate boards are more intense than ever. *The Economist*. https://www.economist.com/business/2023/02/23/demands-on-corporate-boards-are-more-intense-than-ever/

The Economist. (2023b, March 31). A zero-tolerance approach to talented jerks in the workplace is risky. *The Economist*. https://www.economist.com/business/2023/03/30/a-zero-tolerance-approach-to-talented-jerks-in-the-workplace-is-risky

The top 5 ways to spot a toxic workplace. (2021, December 13). Professional Alternatives. https://www.proalt.com/the-top-5-ways-to-spot-a-toxic-workplace/

Top ten signs of a dysfunctional board of directors. (2017, November 21). Small Business – Chron.com. https://smallbusiness.chron.com/top-ten-signs-dysfunctional-board-directors-35728.html

Trump, D., & Zanker, B. (2007). *Think big and kick ass in business and life*.

UK Parliament – Churchill and the Commons Chamber. (n.d.). https://www.parliament.uk/about/living-heritage/building/palace/architecture/palacestructure/churchill/

Van Reken, R. E., Pollock, M. V., & Pollock, D. C. (2017). Third Culture Kids 3rd edition: Growing up among worlds. *Nicholas Brealey*.

Warmspace – Feel Human Again. (n.d.). Warmspace. https://warmspace.io/

Waters, R., & Chon, G. (2015, September 25). Carly Fiorina faces heat over US business record. *Financial Times.* https://www.ft.com/content/bff80858-6397-11e5-9846-de406ccb37f2

Wayne, M. (2022, October 10). Exclusive interview with Carly Fiorina: I was overlooked and dismissed. *CEO Magazine.*

Whicker, M. L. (1996). *Toxic leaders: When organizations go bad.* Praeger.

Why Elon Musk fired his long-term assistant who asked for a raise – Educator.com Blog. (n.d.). https://www.educator.com/news/why-elon-musk-fired-his-long-term-assistant-who-asked-for-a-raise/

WikiJob. (2023). Psychometric tests – Everything you need to know 2023 – Psychometric success. *psychometric-success.com.* https://psychometric-success.com/aptitude-tests/test-types/psychometric-tests

Williams, R. (2012, April 12). Why Steve Jobs is not the leader to emulate. *The Financial Post.*

Wong, J. C. (2017, July 14). Uber CEO Travis Kalanick resigns following months of chaos. *The Guardian.* https://www.theguardian.com/technology/2017/jun/20/uber-ceo-travis-kalanick-resigns

WorldWork. (2022, August 11). *Home – WorldWork.* https://worldwork.global/

INDEX

Printed in the USA
CPSIA information can be obtained
at www.ICGtesting.com
JSHW010810090124
54981JS00007B/12